The Autistic Teen's Avoidant Eating Workbook

of related interest

The Autism-Friendly Cookbook
Lydia Wilkins
ISBN 978 1 83997 082 5
eISBN 978 1 83997 083 2

The Spectrum Girl's Survival Guide
How to Grow Up Awesome and Autistic
Siena Castellon
Foreword by Dr. Temple Grandin
ISBN 978 1 78775 183 5
eISBN 978 1 78775 184 2

My Anxiety Handbook
Getting Back on Track
Sue Knowles, Bridie Gallagher and Phoebe McEwen
Illustrated by Emmeline Pidgen
ISBN 978 1 78592 440 8
eISBN 978 1 78450 813 5

by the same author

Food Refusal and Avoidant Eating in Children,
including those with Autism Spectrum Conditions
A Practical Guide for Parents and Professionals
Gillian Harris and Elizabeth Shea
ISBN 978 1 78592 318 0
eISBN 978 1 78450 632 2

The Autistic Teen's Avoidant Eating Workbook

DR ELIZABETH SHEA

Illustrated by Tim Stringer

Jessica Kingsley Publishers
London and Philadelphia

First published in Great Britain in 2024 by Jessica Kingsley Publishers
An imprint of John Murray Press

1

A CIP catalogue record for this title is available from the
British Library and the Library of Congress

ISBN 978 1 78775 859 9
eISBN 978 1 78775 860 5

Printed and bound in Great Britain by TJ Books Ltd

Jessica Kingsley Publishers' policy is to use papers that are natural,
renewable and recyclable products and made from wood grown in
sustainable forests. The logging and manufacturing processes are expected
to conform to the environmental regulations of the country of origin.

Jessica Kingsley Publishers
Carmelite House
50 Victoria Embankment
London EC4Y 0DZ

www.jkp.com

John Murray Press
Part of Hodder & Stoughton Limited
An Hachette UK Company

To Rachel (aka the 'Wotsit girl'). You taught me so much about the eating issues that autistic teenagers face, and your story has helped so many other young people and their families. You will always be an inspiration to me.

To my parents, Pete and Mary Shea, with love and gratitude.

No day shall erase you from the memory of time.

Contents

Acknowledgements

To Asher for taking the time to read and comment on my drafts of the book: a huge thank you.

To all the young people whose stories and ideas have taught me so much and who were brave enough to trust me: you are amazing.

To all my colleagues in the training, education and conference departments at the National Autistic Society, particularly Lorraine McAllister; thank you for supporting my work and for helping me get the messages out there about avoidant eating in autistic and neurodivergent people.

Notes on the Text

Throughout the book, I use the term 'autistic teenager/teen' when referring to young people with the diagnostic label of 'autism'. This reflects research on the preferences of autistic people about the language used to describe them, which has identified the importance of identity-first descriptions. I also use the terms 'neurodivergent' and 'neurodiverse' when describing individuals and groups of people with autism or with other differences (see Introduction for an explanation). This recognises the importance of 'difference' rather than 'disability' or 'disorder'. These terms are used interchangeably but with recognition that there is no one term that describes everyone.

Similarly, I use the term 'avoidant eating' and the diagnostic label 'ARFID' to describe the common food and eating issues autistic and neurodivergent people have. This is based on my clinical experience that suggests these terms can be useful to help young people understand and explain their eating issues. I fully recognise that they may not describe everyone.

All the stories in the book come from my experience of working with teens with food issues. Any identifying details have been changed for confidentiality.

Who Is This Book for and How Can It Help?

Who is this book for?

This is a book for teenagers and young people who have difficulties with food. It is especially for those of you who are autistic[1] or neurodivergent[2] (I'll explain what these terms mean a bit later on) and who have difficulties eating different kinds of foods. We call this 'avoidant eating'.

Let's begin with a story.

---

1 Being autistic is a spectrum condition and affects people in different ways. Autism usually means people have differences in their social communication/interaction skills, their ability to think flexibly and their sensory processing.

2 The term 'neurodivergent' comes from the idea of 'neurodiversity', which is that there are many ways in which humans think, learn and relate to others and all are equally valuable. Neurodivergent is used to describe one person and neurodiversity to describe a group of people who might be similar.

Rachel only ate four things. These were: milk chocolate, cereal with melted chocolate on top, chocolate finger biscuits and cheesy puff crisps. To the surprise of everyone, including doctors, Rachel was growing, was healthy and was doing well at school. However, Rachel was fed up with what she was eating and wanted to change – in her words, to 'stop it getting in the way of my life'.

Over time, Rachel learnt why she was stuck on these four foods and made positive changes to her eating with the right help, tools and support. You'll learn more about how Rachel (and other young people like her) changed their eating as you read and work through this book. Hopefully, this will enable you to make some changes too.

So, this book is for you if:

1. You are in your teens and you have food issues, particularly if you are autistic or neurodivergent.

2. Your issues with food include all or some of these:

    → There are lots of foods you can't eat.

    → You don't like the way many foods look, feel, smell or taste.

    → You stick to the same 'safe' foods all the time.

    → You don't like to try new foods and think new foods are scary or disgusting.

    → You don't always know if you are hungry or full.

➤ You don't like to eat with other people.

➤ You have routines and rituals around mealtimes that you stick to.

And...

3. You want to change your eating, but you don't know how.

This last point is really important because this book is about helping you start a journey of change. This is your book (even if an adult bought it for you) and you are in charge of whether you even want to read it, and if you do, whether you want to complete the worksheets or follow the ideas and advice it contains. This is your 'self-help' book to use and dip in and out of in the ways you find most helpful for you.

What is neurodiversity?

There are many different kinds of tree. Some are tall, some are small, some lose their leaves in the autumn, others keep them all winter. Some trees only grow in hot climates, others need colder weather. No one kind of tree is better than another; they are just different, and all trees are equally valuable.

This is how it is in humans, too. There are differences or variations in the way that people think, learn and relate to others. This is called 'neurodiversity' and it is often used to describe groups of people with labels such as autism, ADHD,[3] dyslexia and dyspraxia.[4] Individuals who identify in this way or have one of these labels may call themselves 'neurodivergent'. It is thought that one in ten people are neurodivergent in some way. Being neurodivergent might mean being better or worse at some things than other people – you might have amazing strengths and also areas that are more challenging for you. Whatever our differences, just like trees, we are all equally valuable.

Who is this book not for?

Remember, this book is written for young people; it is not written for adults. If you want to show it to a trusted adult, perhaps so they can understand and support you, that's great, but you can work through this book by yourself; you are in charge.

This book may not be right for everyone. Young people can sometimes have eating problems that need more help than just a book can provide.

So this book may not be right for you if any of the following points apply:

---

3   ADHD stands for Attention Deficit Hyperactivity Disorder. People with ADHD can seem restless, may have trouble concentrating and may act on impulse.

4   Dyslexia is a specific learning difficulty where people may have difficulties with reading and writing. Dyspraxia affects people's coordination skills such as appearing to be clumsy.

★ You are losing a lot of weight or becoming ill because of your eating.

★ You are deliberately trying to lose weight by dieting or exercising a lot.

★ You make yourself sick or go to the toilet to get rid of food.

★ You think you look fat even though other people tell you that you are thin.

★ You hide your eating problems from others.

★ You don't think there is anything wrong with your eating or that you need help.

If any of these points do apply to you, then it is really important that you tell a trusted adult, such as a parent or family member, a teacher or health professional. That will be the first step in getting the help you need.

Health and safety warning

This book does not cover food hypersensitivity, food allergies or intolerances. These are a combination of reactions to different foods that range from relatively mild such as stomach pain or itchy skin/rash to very severe such as difficulties breathing and even death. These issues often start in childhood (but not always) and if any of these apply to you (or you think they might), then it is extremely important you talk to a health professional experienced in these problems before trying any of the ideas in this book, particularly trying something new for the first time. If you are in any doubt or are worried that you have unusual reactions to certain foods, then talk to a trusted adult as soon as possible and before reading any more of this book.

How can this book help?

This book will help you to:

1. understand why you have issues with food

2. enable you to make changes to your eating.

This book has seven chapters, each covering a different topic. Each chapter is structured in a similar way so you can easily keep track of what you are learning. Each chapter contains the following:

★ reminders and summaries to help you remember what you have learnt so far

★ stories from other young people that you can relate to

★ worksheets to help you learn about your eating issues and how to change

★ top tips of useful hacks to help you get started or keep going

★ fact finders to help you learn the 'science' of eating

★ illustrations to help you understand and keep you entertained!

Reading the chapters in the order they appear in the book will mean you get the right information at the right time to make changes at your pace.

Here is a summary of what each chapter contains:

Chapter 1: Why Do I Have Issues with Food and Eating?

Chapter 1 explains why some autistic and neurodivergent teenagers have avoidant eating and other issues with food. It explains why having sensory sensitivities, anxiety about food and eating and cognitive differences all affect eating. This chapter introduces the label ARFID[5] to describe some of these issues. This chapter will enable you to identify and start to understand your own food and eating issues.

Chapter 2: Am I Ready to Change My Eating?

Chapter 2 explains how to know if you are ready to change your eating. It explores why being a teenager is the ideal time to start and when is the right and wrong time to begin any change. This chapter will help you decide whether you are ready to make changes and where you can begin.

Chapter 3: Managing My Sensory Differences with Food and Eating

Chapter 3 explains more about why sensory differences are so important in avoidant eating. It covers the senses you've probably heard of such as sight, touch, smell, taste and hearing but also those you may not have heard of such as interoception. Chapter 3 includes ideas to help you reduce your sensory food issues.

---

5   ARFID stands for Avoidant and Restrictive Food Intake Disorder.

Chapter 4: Managing My Anxiety about Food and Eating

Chapter 4 explains how anxiety and stress can cause avoidant eating. It will explore more about why new foods can be scary and why mealtimes can be so stressful. This chapter will give you tips and advice on reducing your anxiety in order to make eating easier for you.

Chapter 5: How to Try a New Food

Chapter 5 explains how to try a new food for the first time. This might sound scary, but this chapter brings together ideas from the previous chapters to give you a step-by-step plan. This starts with helping you choose which food to try and ends with how to make that food a regular one for you.

Chapter 6: How to Eat with Other People

Chapter 6 explains why avoidant eating makes it hard to eat with other people and why social eating situations such as going to a restaurant are often avoided. This chapter will enable you to explain your avoidant eating and gives you strategies to help you learn to eat more easily with other people.

Chapter 7: Managing My Eating when I'm Older

Chapter 7 is about growing up and becoming more independent with food and eating. This chapter will enable you to manage your avoidant eating away from home such as at college/university or work. It will also cover how to stay healthy and cope with buying and preparing your own food when you are an adult. Chapter 7 also explains how other people can help and support you.

At the end of the book, you'll find an Appendix with some of the worksheets you can copy – or download here: www.jkp.com/catalogue/book/9781787758599. Also at the end of the book are a list of references, a glossary (a list of some of the technical words used in the book and what they mean) and a list of organisations that can help with eating issues.

Who is this book written by?

My name is Elizabeth Shea and I work as a clinical psychologist.[6] I've written this book because I've spent many years working with people of all ages who have issues with avoidant eating.

Many of these people are autistic or neurodivergent. I've learnt that eating difficulties can be very hard for those people and their families (can you imagine another difficulty that happens as often as eating?). I've also learnt that there needs to be more information about why these issues happen and what can be done to help.

I've already written one book about avoidant eating for parents, carers and professionals. This book is just for young people themselves. My intention is that it supports

---

6   Clinical psychologists generally help and support people who have health or mental health issues, often in the National Health Service (NHS) in the UK.

you to see that your eating pattern is not your fault. This is a workbook that will empower you to learn the skills for change. Most of all, it will give you the confidence to believe, just like Rachel, that you can make the changes you want. Good luck and happy reading!

Why Do I Have Issues with Food and Eating?

Reminder of what we learnt in the introduction:

* ★ This book is for teenagers with avoidant eating, especially if you are autistic or neurodivergent.

* ★ This book is for you if you want to make changes to your eating.

* ★ This book is not for teenagers whose eating problems are making them very thin or ill.

* ★ This book is not for adults, although it's OK to show the book to an adult.

* ★ This book will help you understand your eating pattern and explain it to others.

* ★ This book will give you ideas to enable you to make changes to your eating.

Introduction

It felt like someone understood us, and the more we learnt about the research, the more it made sense. We began to understand our problem. (Rachel)

This chapter explains why some teenagers, particularly autistic or neurodivergent ones, have avoidant eating issues. The aim of this chapter is to help you understand more about avoidant eating. As Rachel says, understanding what causes avoidant eating is really important as it is the first step to making any changes.

In this chapter you will discover:

- ★ that avoidant eating is common in autistic and neurodivergent people

- ★ more about your own eating and food issues

- ★ how to keep a food diary and why you eat what you do

- ★ more about the science of eating

- ★ why sensory sensitivity, anxiety and cognitive differences can cause avoidant eating

- ★ how the label ARFID can help you understand and describe your eating.

Eating issues are really common in autism (nobody has researched how many neurodivergent people have eating issues so we don't know that yet). Scientists think that as many as half of autistic people have some kind of food problem, and it may even be more. This is much more than people who are not autistic. So if you ever thought it was 'just me', then you are not alone; other autistic teenagers have similar issues with food.

Worksheet 1.1 will help you see which of your food and eating issues are similar to other people.

Chapter 1 Worksheet 1.1: My Food and Eating Issues

Below is a list of things autistic and neurodivergent people say about their eating.

Read the list and tick (✓) the ones that are true for you.

You can write down any other eating issues you have at the end.

1. I only eat a very few foods ☐

2. I don't like the way many foods look, feel, smell or taste ☐

3. I struggle to eat if it's noisy ☐

4. I can't tell when I am hungry or full ☐

5. I find a lot of foods disgusting ☐

6. I don't like it when different foods touch each other or are mixed together ☐

7. New foods make me anxious and I don't like trying them ☐

8. I don't like eating with other people ☐

9. I stick to the same foods most days ☐

10. I have set routines and rituals which I must do around foods or mealtimes ☐

My other eating issues:

1. . . . .

2. . . . .

How many did you tick? I'm guessing a few – maybe even all. That's because most autistic and neurodivergent teenagers have similar food and eating issues. This includes only eating a few safe foods, finding sensory things (such as taste and smell) hard, and avoiding trying any new foods. That's why the term 'avoidant eating' is so useful because it describes exactly what most people do when they have this eating issue.

Did you notice there was a pattern in what you ticked on Worksheet 1.1? If so, that's because avoidant eating is usually caused by three things:

1. sensory 'differences'

2. anxiety and stress

3. cognitive[1] 'differences'.

Let's explain why these happen one by one.

Sensory differences

Our sensory systems are essential for eating. Without our senses we wouldn't know when to eat, what is safe to eat and what we like. Without our senses eating would basically be impossible!

---

1   Cognitive is another word for the brain processes of thinking, reasoning (making sense of things) and remembering.

Fact Finder 1.1: How many senses?

Our sensory systems are unique to each of us. Most people think we have five senses which are:

1. auditory – our sense of hearing

2. gustatory – our sense of taste

3. olfactory – our sense of smell

4. tactile – our sense of touch

5. vision – our sense of sight.

Did you know that science tells us we actually have at least eight senses! The others are:

6. interoception – our sense of how our body feels inside (e.g. whether we are hungry)

7. proprioception – our sense of where our body is (e.g. standing up or sitting down)

8. vestibular – our sense of balance (e.g. riding a bicycle).

All of our senses play a part in eating – even proprioception. For example, you can't eat properly or safely if you're not sitting or standing upright.

Sensory 'differences' are a big part of autism and neurodiversity. These include being extra or less sensitive to things than non-autistic/non-neurodivergent people.

Read Stephan's story and see if you can identify what his sensory differences are.

Stephan likes toast but it has to be the exact shade of brown or it isn't 'right'. Stephan can't eat in the dining room at school when it is busy, and he feels sick when other people sit near him and eat. Stephan says that some foods feel 'painful' in his mouth.

Did you identify any of Stephan's sensory differences and are any of these similar to yours?

Stephan is extra sensitive to:

* ★ the way foods look – that's why his toast has to be the right shade of brown

* ★ noise – that's why he can't eat in the dining room at school when it is busy

* ★ smell – that's why other people's food makes him feel sick

* ★ texture – that's why some foods feel painful in his mouth.

Now, read Raj's story and see if you can identify what his sensory differences are.

Raj likes foods with a strong taste like garlic and really sour-tasting sweets/candy. Raj really likes crunchy foods, and he can't tell when he is full.

Did you identify any of Raj's sensory differences and are any of these similar to yours?

Raj is less sensitive to:

- ★ taste – that's why he seeks really strong or sour flavours

- ★ texture – that's why he seeks crunchy foods

- ★ interoception – that's why he can't tell when he is full.

Many people with avoidant eating find they are extra sensitive to some things and less sensitive to others. Everyone's sensory system is unique, and Chapter 3 will help you understand yours better.

So sensory differences are important in what foods are eaten or avoided. Let's look at what people with avoidant eating often choose to eat and why:

- ★ Beige (light brown) foods (e.g. bread, biscuits, crisps, crackers, cereal, fries, pasta).

  Hint: These foods look similar and are easy if you are sensitive to sight.

- ★ Smooth foods with no bits or lumps (e.g. yoghurt, cream cheese, smoothies).

  Hint: These foods are easy if you are sensitive to texture.

- ★ Sweet foods (e.g. sweets, chocolate, puddings).

  Hint: These foods are easy if you are sensitive to taste (babies are born liking sweet tastes).

★ Branded foods (e.g. from the right shop, restaurant or manufacturer).

Hint: These foods always look the same and are easy if you are sensitive to sight.

Let's look at what foods are often avoided and why:

★ Fruits and vegetables – these look different and have tricky textures and tastes.

★ Meat – these have tricky textures unless mashed into a nugget or sausage.

★ Fish – these have strong smells but may be OK if made into fish fingers.

★ Foods mixed together – these have confusing textures, smells and tastes.

Autistic and neurodivergent people generally only eat foods that look, feel, smell and **taste** right to them and they avoid foods that don't look, feel, smell or taste right. This makes total sense! Chapter 3 will help you understand your sensory differences and how you can begin to manage these to change your eating.

> ## Top Tip: Not right for me
>
> Next time someone offers you a food that doesn't look, feel, smell or taste right for you, instead of saying 'I don't like it', explain that your sensory sensitivities make this too hard for you. That will help them understand why you have problems with food.

Our sensory systems also protect us from eating anything that isn't safe. This is what disgust is for. Disgust is a brain signal that protects us from eating anything dangerous, such as something that might poison us or make us sick. Autistic and neurodivergent people are often extra sensitive to disgust. This means they find many foods, even those that other people like, disgusting and don't eat them. Some people are so extra sensitive they vomit just looking at a food. This is another reason autistic and neurodivergent people stick to the same 'safe' foods and have difficulties sitting near people eating other foods.

Top Tip: Understanding your disgust

Next time you feel disgusted by a food, stop and think whether it is the look, feel, smell or taste that is triggering your disgust. This will give you clues about which foods you can try in the future and which foods will be more difficult for you.

Disgust has a twin called 'contamination'.

Read more of Stephan's story.

Stephan hated it when his safe foods touched foods he didn't like. Stephan's mum once mixed grated carrot with grated cheese. Stephan spotted the carrot straight away and then couldn't eat the cheese any more.

Does Stephan's story sound familiar? Contamination is where a new food touches a safe food and makes it 'unsafe'. Contamination is another brain signal designed to protect us from eating anything dangerous. A good example of contamination is what happens if we drop food on the floor; most people would throw it away rather than carry on eating. This is because the food could be contaminated by dirt on the floor.

Contamination is why if anyone has ever hidden another food in your safe food, you've probably, like Stephan, spotted it and then not eaten your safe food. This is because we lose trust when other people try to hide things in our food. Usually, people do it because they are worried about avoidant eating and they think it will help you eat different foods. Now you can explain to them why this doesn't work!

The slug sandwich

Imagine I have made your favourite sandwich. It looks great; you start eating and then you take a bite of a big fat slug hidden away in the sandwich! Urgh! What do you do? Spit it out? Feel sick? Perhaps you even vomit. This is what disgust feels like.

Would you still eat the rest of the sandwich once you'd got rid of the slug? Probably not; in fact, you would probably throw it all away. This is what contamination feels like.

Perhaps you'll never eat a sandwich again. You'll definitely never let me make you one!

Our senses also help us recognise when we are hungry and when we are full. The brain signal that controls this is called 'appetite'. Many autistic and neurodivergent people don't notice appetite because of differences in interoception. This means they may go a long time without eating or drinking or may eat too much, both of which can be dangerous.

The good news is that even without noticing appetite, many autistic and neurodivergent people often manage to eat just the right amount for them. Chapter 3 will explain how to recognise the signs of appetite.

Let's talk now about the role of anxiety and stress in avoidant eating.

Anxiety and stress

Imagine I've put a new food in front of you and asked you to try it. How do you feel?

Read other young people's responses and then write your answer in the blank speech bubble:

> I can't. It's too scary!

> I couldn't. It's too hard!

If you wrote that this would be too hard or make you anxious, you are not alone; many other autistic and neurodivergent teenagers also find trying new foods difficult. Why?

All young children go through a stage where they are anxious about new foods. This is called 'neophobia'[2] and is another brain signal designed to protect children from eating anything new that might be dangerous. As children grow up, neophobia goes away; this is because children learn which foods are safe by watching others eat.

Fact Finder 1.2: Survival of the fittest

Scientists think neophobia has been around for thousands of years. Along with disgust and contamination, it helped early humans stay safe when they hunted and gathered their food. Anyone who ate something new that no one else had eaten before might have died, so neophobia actually helped humans to survive.

So if anyone ever says you are 'weird' because you can't try a new food, tell them about neophobia and that this means you have the best survival skills!

---

2   Neophobia comes from the Ancient Greek for 'fear of the new'.

Many autistic and neurodivergent teens find that neophobia didn't go away as they grew up and they are still anxious about trying anything new. If this is you, then don't worry. The good news is that as you enter your teens, it actually becomes easier to overcome neophobia. Chapters 4 and 5 will give you some ideas about how to do this.

Let's talk about mealtimes now. What are these like for you? Do you hate sitting with other people? Does the sight and smell of other foods make you feel disgusted? Are you worried someone will make you eat something you don't want to eat? Do you want to run away? Is it easier if you can eat by yourself?

Write down any of your thoughts about mealtimes in the bubbles:

Many autistic and neurodivergent people find mealtimes difficult. This is because being with other people and social interactions can be hard, and too much sensory information can cause sensory 'overload'. This is where too much sensory information comes in for your brain and body to cope with. Sensory overload causes shutdown, panic and anxiety. Chapter 4 will explain more about the impact of anxiety and stress on avoidant eating and help you manage this. Chapter 6 will help you learn how to eat with other people and reduce sensory overload to make mealtimes more enjoyable.

Anxiety and stress also cause autistic and neurodivergent people to find it hard to think clearly or remember things. These are called 'cognitive differences' and they also affect eating. Let's talk about this next.

Cognitive differences

Most autistic and some neurodivergent people dislike change and prefer when things are familiar. Researchers think this is because the autistic or neurodivergent brain can take more time to get used to new information or situations. As a result, new things can make an autistic or neurodivergent person anxious.

> ### Fact Finder 1.3: Autistic and neurodivergent brains
>
> So, how do our brains actually work? Scientists are still trying to figure this out. It's a pretty big question!
>
> We do know that autistic and neurodivergent people have some differences in how they think, make sense of and remember things. Some of these differences can be very helpful, such as the ability to focus incredibly well on something you find interesting, but some of them can affect eating.

For example:

- preferring familiar things – this may mean you stick to the same foods

- remembering past events (e.g. remembering a disgust experience from long ago)

- spotting small details (e.g. the toast being the wrong shade of brown)

- being very focused on something interesting – this may mean you forget to eat.

Some autistic and neurodivergent people manage these cognitive differences by sticking to familiar things, doing the same things over and over (called routines) or behaving in ways to feel in control (called rituals).

Maryam is autistic; read her story.

Maryam eats the same two foods for lunch every day. She can only eat if she has a yellow plate. Lunch has to be at exactly 12.30. Maryam eats in the same chair watching the same TV programme. If any of these things change, Maryam becomes very anxious and can't eat.

Maryam is trying to make mealtimes more familiar by eating the same foods, having a routine of eating lunch at the same time and the ritual of always using a yellow plate. These reduce her anxiety. This is OK, but sometimes routines and rituals get out of control; in Maryam's case, she is stuck because she can't eat without them. Chapter 4 will give you some alternative ideas about how to manage anxiety around food and mealtimes.

One of the things Maryam does is eat the same foods every day. Let's find out whether you do this too by completing a food diary.

Chapter 1 Worksheet 1.2: My Food Diary

1. Use the template below to make a list of **every** food you eat for the **next 3 days**.

2. Now, count **how many** different foods you have eaten.

   Hint: Different brands or flavours count as separate foods, so if you eat 2 flavours of crisp then that counts as 2 foods.

3. Put a star (*) next to your 'safest' foods and write why they are safe.

Day 1

Breakfast: ....

Lunch: ....

Dinner/tea: ....

Snacks/drinks: ....

Day 2

Breakfast: ....

Lunch: ....

Dinner/tea: ....

Snacks/drinks: ....

Day 3

    Breakfast: . . . .

    Lunch: . . . .

    Dinner/tea: . . . .

    Snacks/drinks: . . . .

Total number of foods: . . . .

My safe foods are safe because: . . . .

. . . .

There is a blank copy of this worksheet in Appendix 1 that you can use again.

How many different foods did you count? My guess is less than 20 different foods. Can you see any patterns in what you eat? Generally, autistic and some neurodivergent people eat fewer foods than other people, and you may also often eat the same foods every day and eat foods that are similar to each other.

Top Tip: Choosing a new food

Making a list of what you eat now will really help you in Chapter 5 where we will talk about how to try something new. Knowing what you already eat and why will help you choose something new to try.

We are almost at the end of the first chapter of the book. Before we finish, I want to introduce the label 'ARFID' for describing the eating issues we have talked about. Many young people find this label helps them understand their eating issues and describe them to others.

Fact Finder 1.4: What is ARFID?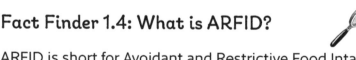

ARFID is short for Avoidant and Restrictive Food Intake Disorder. It is a new label and includes these three features:

1. Not being interested in eating or food (e.g. not noticing appetite or enjoying eating).

2. Avoiding foods due to sensory characteristics (e.g. the look, feel, smell and taste).

3. Worries about what happens when eating (e.g. anxiety, disgust, being sick).

Some people with ARFID also:

- lose weight and lack the right vitamins and minerals for good health

- need to be fed by a tube – this is very rare

- find their eating causes problems in their daily life – this is really common.

ARFID is:

- different to not being given food – this is called neglect

- different to fasting – this is not eating as part of religious beliefs

- different to eating disorders – this is deliberately not eating to be extremely thin or to change body shape.

Do any of the features of ARFID apply to you? If so, you are in the right place reading this book. ARFID is a new label, and scientists are still learning about it. Just like autism or neurodiversity, ARFID is different for everyone. We do know that ARFID does seem to be more common for autistic or neurodivergent people. If you would like to know more, such as whether you actually have ARFID, then talk to a trusted adult.

As ARFID is a relatively new label, there are still not very many NHS services available in the UK (if you are reading this book in another country, then this might be different). Hopefully, this will change as more health professionals learn and understand about ARFID and more people with avoidant eating talk about what it is like for them.

Here are some tips for getting a diagnosis and for finding more support:

1. In the first instance, go to your general practitioner (GP) or family doctor and explain your eating to them.

   Hint: It can be useful to take with you some information about ARFID as many doctors are still not aware of it yet.

2. If you are an adult with a child or teenager under the age of 18 with possible ARFID, then these health professionals may be able to make a diagnosis of ARFID:

   → Paediatrician – a medical doctor specialising in child/adolescent physical health.

   → Child and adolescent psychiatrist – a medical doctor specialising in mental health.

   → Child clinical psychologist – supports anxiety and mental health.

   Hint: It is possible to see adult (over 18) specialists within these professions, too.

3. Ask your GP or health professional what support is available for ARFID in your area. If there are no services yet, don't be afraid to ask why not. Often services start

when people with lived experience of a condition such as ARFID ask or campaign for more support.

Hint: You may find joining a social media site or online community connects you with other people with ARFID or avoidant eating. These can be helpful for hearing other people's experiences and finding out about services and supports. Check with your GP before beginning any kind of 'treatment' from a non-NHS service to make sure it is OK.

Finally, Chapter 7 of this book gives information about UK national organisations that can support individuals or families with ARFID.

For the rest of the book, I will continue to use 'avoidant eating' and 'ARFID' to describe the food and eating issues autistic and neurodivergent people have. Hopefully, this will help you, although I understand that it may not describe everyone who reads this book.

Now we've got to the end of Chapter 1, what have we learnt?

Summary of Chapter 1

✓ Avoidant eating issues are common in autistic and neurodivergent teens and young people.

✓ Eating a few foods and avoiding foods that don't look, feel, smell or taste OK are common.

✓ Sensory differences, anxiety and cognitive differences all cause eating issues.

✓ Sensory differences include being extra or less sensitive to foods.

✓ Many people with avoidant eating are extra sensitive to disgust and contamination.

✓ Sensory overload can make mealtimes difficult.

✓ Neophobia makes trying new foods hard for autistic and neurodivergent people.

✓ Routines and rituals about food and eating can be a way of coping with anxiety.

✓ Making a food diary can help you understand your eating.

✓ ARFID describes some autistic and neurodivergent people's eating.

Am I Ready to Change My Eating?

Reminder of what we learnt in Chapter 1:

★ Avoidant eating issues are common in autistic and neurodivergent teenagers.

★ Eating a few foods and avoiding foods that don't look, feel, smell or taste OK are common.

★ Sensory differences, anxiety and cognitive differences all cause eating issues.

★ Sensory differences include being extra or less sensitive to foods.

★ Many people with avoidant eating are extra sensitive to disgust and contamination.

★ Sensory overload can make mealtimes difficult.

★ Neophobia makes trying new foods hard for autistic and neurodivergent people.

★ Routines and rituals about food and eating can be a way of coping with anxiety.

★ Making a food diary can help you understand your eating.

★ ARFID describes some autistic and neurodivergent people's eating.

Introduction

Change for me didn't happen overnight; patience is a virtue! But I wanted to be healthy, have choices and to fit in. (Rachel)

In this chapter we will explore being ready to change your eating pattern. This may be the most important chapter in this book because unless you are ready, most of the ideas, strategies and techniques described in later chapters simply won't work. It's a good sign you are still reading as this suggests you do want to make some changes!

The aim of this chapter is to help you understand if you are ready and what to do next.

In this chapter you will discover:

★ when not to make changes

★ how to manage worries about change

★ how to understand where you are in the 'change cycle'

★ how to spot the signs you are ready

★ how 'motivation' helps you change

★ how to set goals and track your progress

★ how to make a plan for change.

By the end of this chapter, you will have a good understanding of whether you are ready to make changes and, if so, where to start.

When not to make changes

It might sound strange to start a chapter about being ready for change by looking at when not to make changes! However, this is really important as there are times in everyone's life that can cause extra stress and anxiety, and this can stop you eating even your safe foods. Chapter 4 will explain more about how stress and anxiety impact on eating. As a general rule, any situation or period of time where your usual routines are interrupted can be extra challenging when it comes to making a change with food.

Chapter 2 Worksheet 2.1: My Stressful Times

This is a list of possible stressful times or events. Tick (✓) all that apply to you and write how they might impact on you. Add any other times or events at the end.

1. Exam time
   Impact ....

2. Start or end of a school/college term or half-term
   Impact ....

3. September or the start of a new school/college year
   Impact ....

4. Going on holiday
   Impact ....

5. Cultural or religious holidays (e.g. Christmas)
   Impact ....

6. Big family events (e.g. moving house, someone leaving home)
   Impact ....

7. Other transitions (e.g. leaving school)
   Impact ....

8. Being physically or mentally unwell
   Impact ....

Other stressful times or events for me:

1. ....

2. ....

Doing a list like this shouldn't put you off considering change. Instead, it can help you plan when to begin and give you a good structure and timetable for what you will do next. Picking the right time to begin gives you the best possible start.

It can be hard to know when to start making changes to your eating. Here are some examples of when other young people have decided to start:

Joe wanted to eat out in a restaurant with friends on his birthday. He began to plan where he would go and what he would eat a couple of months before.

Fatima began trying a new food after her exams finished.

Alex didn't like the changes to routines at school at Christmas. They decided to wait until the end of January before changing anything.

Faizan had planned to try a new food in school in the middle of term, but he had a cold, so he put it off for a couple of weeks and started when he was better.

Knowing what the barriers might be for you and making a plan around these will really help you make a good start. You might also need to be prepared to adapt your plan if something unexpected happens such as getting ill. This is OK – remember the most important thing is that you go at your own pace. This chapter will end with some ideas about how to make a plan.

Managing worries about change

Change is scary for many people, and if you are autistic or neurodivergent, it can be terrifying. This is because it can take longer to adapt and get used to the new situation and is one of the cognitive differences we talked about in Chapter 1.

It really helps to get your worries out of your brain by writing them down. Once you have done this, it also helps to challenge the worry by thinking of a different response that is more positive and empowering. Worksheet 2.2 will help you do this.

Chapter 2 Worksheet 2.2:
My Worries about Change

Read these worries from other young people:

I'll fail and look stupid

What if I hate it?

It's too hard for me

Now write down your own worries in the thought bubbles below. For each worry, try to think of a different response, we call this a 'worry challenge'. Here's an example:

My worry

I'll fail and look stupid

My worry challenge

I might not succeed the first time but I'm just going to try!

My worry

My worry challenge

Well done! Writing down and challenging worries gives your brain another way of thinking about difficult tasks and can help increase your confidence in doing new things. Don't worry if this exercise was hard; we'll talk more about managing anxious and worrying thoughts about food and eating in Chapter 4.

Understanding the Change Cycle

Have you ever made a New Year's resolution? If you have and then not kept it going (which is really common), then you will know that making a change to a behaviour or habit can be hard, especially if it is something you've done for a long time. Knowing how ready you are to make a change will help you succeed. The 'Change Cycle' can help you understand this.

Fact Finder 2.1: The science of change

In the 1980s, scientists James Prochaska and Carlo DiClemente (Prochaska & DiClemente, 1983) invented what is known as the 'Change Cycle' to help people change unwanted habits. They identified six stages that people go through when making a change to their behaviour:

1. Precontemplation – *I don't need to change.*

2. Contemplation – *I am thinking about change.*

3. Preparation – *I am working on how to change.*

4. Action – *I am working on my change.*

5. Maintenance – *I am keeping my change going.*

6. Relapse – *I've gone backwards and need to start again.*

(Adapted from Prochaska and DeClimente, 1983)

Since it was invented, the Change Cycle has been used by psychologists and other therapists to enable people to identify how ready they are for a change and to help them keep going.

The Change Cycle recognises that different people might be at different stages in their journey to making a change. It also allows for the possibility of 'relapse' where we might slip back to previous stages. Sometimes we have a setback – this is OK. The secret is to go back to the stage of the cycle that feels right and start again from there.

Diagram 2.1 shows what the Change Cycle looks like if we use it to make a change to eating.

We are going to use it in Worksheet 2.3 to help you see where you are right now in the Change Cycle.

Diagram 2.1: The Change Cycle and eating

Chapter 2 Worksheet 2.3: The Change Cycle, Eating and Me

1. Look at Diagram 2.1 which shows the Change Cycle and eating. The example used is trying toast, but you can use it for any change.

2. Think of a change you want to make to your eating in the future. Write it here:

    ....

3. Which stage in the Change Cycle do you think you are at right now? Write it here:

    ....

    Hint: Just by reading this book you are already in the 'contemplation' and 'preparation' stages!

Did you identify where you are right now in the Change Cycle? The good news is that just by reading this book, you are already in the 'contemplation' and 'preparation' stages! As these are the stages immediately before you begin a change, you are definitely on the road to being ready.

Spotting the signs of being ready

Rachel was fed up with only eating four things and wanted to change. This is what she said when I asked her why.

I want to have a sleepover for my 14th birthday, but I'm worried my friends will think I'm 'weird' eating chocolate and cheesy puffs for breakfast. I'd really like to be able to eat toast instead, just like my friends do. (Rachel)

Rachel's story contains many of the signs of being ready:

- ★ Being in your teens – getting older means it is easier to make changes.

- ★ Being fed up with what you eat – this helps you add something new.

- ★ Being interested in trying a new food – choosing a food is the first step in trying it.

- ★ Being 'motivated' or having a good reason – this helps you overcome anxiety.

- ★ Having a goal – this helps you plan the steps you need to make.

If any of these signs are true for you, then the good news is you are getting ready to make some changes. Even if none of these are true for you yet, continue to work through this chapter and the rest of the book – hopefully, the information and stories you'll read will inspire you!

How motivation helps change

Motivation means the reason why we might do something. For example, I want to get fit, so I am motivated to ride my bicycle even when it's raining. Having a good reason for doing something increases our chance of success. So having a good reason to want to change your eating is really important as the more motivated you are, the easier it will be. This is because motivation helps reduce anxiety about change.

Here are some examples of motivation to change their eating from other young people:

Amber wanted to try a hamburger so she could eat them on holiday in New York.

Krishnan wanted to eat more vegetables to be healthier.

Charlie wanted to try pizza so he could eat it at his 18th birthday party.

Rani wanted to be able to sit and eat with her family at her sister's wedding.

Being motivated doesn't take away the anxiety completely, but it does help you fight it and hopefully win. Motivation increases with age, particularly in the teenage years, which is why being a teenager is a definite advantage when it comes to changing eating. The other advantage that teens and young people have over other people is that fitting in with friends and peers is usually very important to them. This often means wanting to eat a food because your friends eat it, just like Rachel. This can be an excellent motivator.

Chapter 2 Worksheet 2.4: My Motivators

These are common 'motivators' that teenagers say enable a change to their eating.

Tick (✓) all that apply to you and write any others in the space at the end.

1. Wanting to eat what my friends eat ☐

2. Wanting to eat something new for a special occasion (e.g. a birthday) ☐

3. Wanting to eat a new food for a holiday ☐

4. Wanting to have more choice of foods ☐

5. Wanting to be healthier ☐

6. Wanting to eat with friends (e.g. at a restaurant) ☐

Other motivators for me:

1. . . . .

2. . . . .

The most important thing to say about motivation is that it has to be your reason, not someone else's. Parents are often very motivated for their teenager to change their eating and can put a bit too much pressure on.

Read Dan's story.

Dan wanted to eat peanuts as he liked how they looked. His mum wanted him to eat raisins because they are healthy. Dan thought raisins looked like rabbit poo; Dan didn't try the raisins!

Remember, only you can say when you are ready and what you want to change. We'll pick up how Dan went about trying peanuts in the next section.

Setting goals and tracking progress

Perhaps by now, you are getting closer to being ready. If so, how do you know where to start? This is where setting goals can really help.

A goal isn't just what you might score in football or netball; it can be any result or achievement that you have put some work into. In the same way a player has to aim right to score a goal in football, you will need a clear aim of what you want to change about your eating.

Here are some examples of eating goals from other young people:

Eva is bored of her foods so wants to eat two new things.

Kazem wants to be able to tell when he is hungry.

Freddie wants to go to a restaurant and eat with his friends.

Vashti wants to eat in the college café.

As well as having a clear idea about what you want to change, you will also need to have a plan about how you will get there. This is where SMART goals can help.

A SMART goal breaks down the steps needed to achieve a result. SMART stands for:

- ★ **S**pecific – your goal is clear and you know what you are aiming for.

- ★ **M**easurable – you will know when you have reached your goal.

- ★ **A**chievable – your goal is possible to reach.

- ★ **R**elevant – your goal is really important to you.

- ★ **T**imely – you will reach your goal within a certain time.

Let's demonstrate how to set a SMART goal for eating. For example, Dan's goal is:

I want to be able to try one new food – peanuts.

Here's how Dan might set a SMART goal to achieve this:

1. **S**pecific – Dan to decide exactly what sort of peanuts he will try (e.g. salted/plain).

2. **M**easurable – Dan to set times for trying peanuts and record what he thinks of them.

3. **A**chievable – Dan to choose the food that is OK for him. **Hint:** Peanuts, not raisins!

4. **R**elevant – Dan to be motivated to eat peanuts (e.g. he can eat them at the cinema).

5. **T**imely – Dan to have a date for eating peanuts regularly (e.g. by his birthday).

The best thing about SMART goals is they break down the steps you need to do to reach your goal, making it less scary.

Have a go now at setting a SMART goal yourself using Worksheet 2.5. If you haven't thought of a goal yet, that's OK; you can either come back to this worksheet when you have thought of one or, for now, make one up. All that matters is that you learn how a SMART goal can break down making a change into easy steps.

Chapter 2 Worksheet 2.5: My SMART Goal

Think of a change you want to make about your eating. This will be your SMART goal.

Write it here:

My goal: . . . .

Now break the goal down by filling in the steps below:

1. **S**pecific: . . . .

2. **M**easurable: . . . .

3. **A**chievable: . . . .

4. **R**elevant: . . . .

5. **T**imely: . . . .

Hint: Keep this worksheet as you will need it later in the book. There is also a blank copy in Appendix 1 that you can use again.

SMART goals also help you track your progress. Keeping a record of how you are doing keeps you motivated and, most importantly, tells you when you have reached your goal!

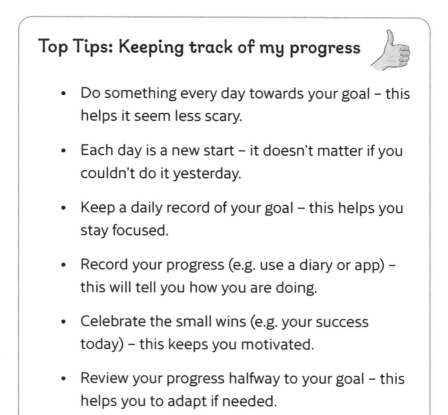

Top Tips: Keeping track of my progress

- Do something every day towards your goal – this helps it seem less scary.

- Each day is a new start – it doesn't matter if you couldn't do it yesterday.

- Keep a daily record of your goal – this helps you stay focused.

- Record your progress (e.g. use a diary or app) – this will tell you how you are doing.

- Celebrate the small wins (e.g. your success today) – this keeps you motivated.

- Review your progress halfway to your goal – this helps you to adapt if needed.

Keeping track means that when you look back over a few days, weeks or even months, you'll be amazed at how much progress you've made without even realising it! When you have a system for keeping track of your progress, you'll always know you're moving in the right direction, no matter how big or difficult the goal is. The more you progress, the more motivated you will be and the more likely you are to succeed. It is also the best way to stop any worries about change that might get in the way.

Making a plan for change

The last section of this chapter will help you put together what you have learnt so far to make a plan for change. This plan is unique to you and will be your road map for the journey ahead. Just like any journey, you can travel at your own speed. It might take time to get to your destination. You can also take breaks and stop for a while or even go in a different direction. Remember, you are in charge of what you change and when.

It's also OK if you are not ready yet. Continuing to read this book will help you plan ahead for the time when you are ready. Everyone reaches the point where they are ready eventually.

Diagram 2.2 shows what a road map for change can look like for trying a new food. You can use this as a template (there is a blank version in Appendix 1) or make your own.

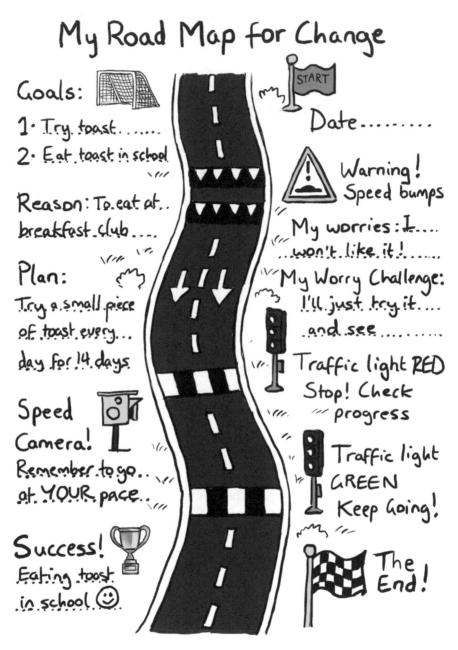

Diagram 2.2: My plan for change

Whatever the template you use, your plan needs to contain the following:

★ Start and finish dates – these will make your plan timely.

★ Your goals – these will make your plan specific.

★ Your reasons for change – these will keep you going.

★ Warnings of any barriers – these will prepare you to overcome them.

★ Reminders to go at your pace – these will help you slow down if you need to.

★ Reminders to check progress – these keep you going in the right direction.

So, how did Rachel manage her plan for change? Read her story.

Rachel's goal was to eat toast for breakfast on her birthday sleepover. She began a month before her birthday. Every other day, she tried a small piece of toast and set an alarm on her phone to remind her. To keep track, she put a tick on a calendar every day she tried toast. Rachel skipped Wednesdays as this was PE day at school which was extra stressful for her. Each week, Rachel looked at the ticks on the calendar so she could see how she was progressing. At the end of the month, Rachel had tried toast 12 times and realised she liked it.

I'm really pleased to tell you that Rachel ate two pieces of toast for breakfast on the morning of her birthday, just as she had planned! I hope Rachel's story shows you that by having a goal, being motivated, making a plan and keeping a track of progress it is possible to make a change to your eating, just like she did.

Now we've got to the end of Chapter 2, what have we learnt?

Summary of Chapter 2

✓ Understanding if you are ready to make a change is the first step.

✓ Understanding when to begin and when not to gives you the best start.

✓ Everyone worries about change, and challenging worries can help.

✓ Reading this book means you are already getting ready in the Change Cycle.

✓ Signs of being ready include being a teenager and wanting to eat something new.

✓ Motivation to change reduces anxiety and makes it easier.

✓ SMART goals break down the steps and help you decide what to change and when.

✓ If you are not ready yet, that's OK – everyone is ready eventually.

✓ Keeping a track of progress helps you stay motivated and keep going.

✓ Making a plan for change gives you a map for your journey to success!

Managing My Sensory Differences with Food and Eating

Reminder of what we learnt in Chapter 2:

★ Understanding if you are ready to make a change is the first step.

★ Understanding when to begin and when not to gives you the best start.

★ Everyone worries about change, and challenging worries can help.

★ Reading this book means you are already getting ready in the Change Cycle.

★ Signs of being ready include being a teenager and wanting to eat something new.

★ Motivation to change reduces anxiety and makes it easier.

★ SMART goals break down the steps and help you decide what to change and when.

★ If you are not ready yet, that's OK – everyone is ready eventually.

★ Keeping a track of progress helps you stay motivated and keep going.

★ Making a plan for change gives you a map for your journey to success!

Introduction

I only like crunchy things; my favourite food is chocolate crispy cake. At birthdays I have a cake but I never try it. I once had a tiny crumb of birthday cake but it made me feel sick. (Rachel)

Does Rachel's story sound familiar? Many autistic or neurodivergent people have sensory differences about foods and eating. Chapter 3 aims to help you understand more about your own sensory food issues, how these cause avoidant eating and how you can learn to manage them.

In this chapter you will discover:

★ more about the sensory differences that autistic or neurodivergent people have with foods

★ more about your own sensory differences with food and eating

★ more about how sight, touch, smell and taste sensitivities cause eating issues

★ how to manage your sensory sensitivities with food one sense at a time

★ how to train your brain to recognise feeling hungry and full.

Remember Dan from Chapter 2? Dan is autistic and also has ARFID. Read more of his story.

Dan's foods had to look exactly right. If the packaging of his chips changed or if the chips were burnt, he couldn't eat them. Dan hated foods with bits, and he smelled all his foods to check they were OK before he ate them. He couldn't eat at college because it was too noisy, and the sights and smells of other people's food made him feel sick. Sometimes Dan would go a whole day without eating anything.

Does Dan's story sound familiar? If so, that's because his story contains many of the common sensory differences that autistic and neurodivergent people have around foods. These also occur in avoidant eating or ARFID.

These sensory differences include:

★ foods have to look exactly right, including the packaging

★ only liking foods of certain textures (e.g. crunchy or smooth)

★ being extra sensitive to smell and taste

★ being extra sensitive to disgust and contamination

★ having sensory overload in noisy or busy dining rooms or restaurants

★ not liking eating with others and avoiding this

★ not noticing being hungry and not eating for a long time

★ not noticing being full and eating too much.

In Chapter 1, we learnt that our sensory system is unique to each of us. Worksheet 3.1 will help you identify what some of your own sensory differences are with foods and eating.

✓

Chapter 3 Worksheet 3.1: My Sensory Differences with Food and Eating

Read the statements below and tick (✓) the ones that apply to you.

To help you, the sense each statement describes is in brackets.

Write down any other sensory issues you have with food at the end.

1. I can't eat foods that don't look right (vision/sight) ☐

2. I can't eat my foods if the packaging changes (vision/sight) ☐

3. I can't touch some foods or put them in my mouth (tactile/touch) ☐

4. I like certain food textures (e.g. crunchy or soft) (tactile/touch) ☐

5. I find many smells unpleasant (olfactory/smell) ☐

6. I smell foods before I taste them (olfactory/smell) ☐

7. I find many tastes unpleasant (gustatory/taste) ☐

8. There are some tastes I seek out or really want (gustatory/taste) ☐

9. Too much noise puts me off eating (auditory/hearing) ☐

10. I can't eat in busy places (auditory/hearing) ☐

11. I can't tell when I'm hungry (interoception) ☐

12. I can't tell when I am full (interoception) ☐

My other sensory differences:

1. . . . .

2. . . . .

How many of the statements in Worksheet 3.1 did you tick and what does it mean?

Here is a quick guide:

★ Ticking 3 or 4 statements means your sensory differences may **sometimes** be an issue.

★ Ticking up to 8 statements means your sensory differences may **often** be an issue.

★ Ticking more than 8 means your sensory differences may **always** be an issue.

I am going to guess that most of you have sensory differences that often or always cause you issues with food and eating. That is because autistic or neurodivergent people are more likely to have sensory differences with foods. They may also have sensory differences that affect other areas of their life. If this is the case for you, then Chapter 7 gives more information about where to get support.

Fact Finder 3.1: The disappearing food

Look at the food diary you made in Chapter 1. Are there any changes since you filled it in? For example, have you eaten anything different or even stopped eating something you've eaten for a long time?

Did you know it is common to suddenly stop eating a food you've eaten for a long time? Scientists have discovered our brains have evolved to like variety. This was essential when humans hunted and gathered their food, because if there was a shortage of one food, then they had to be able to eat other things in order to survive.

Although it is much easier to find food today, our brains still want variety and actually get bored of the look, feel, smell and taste of a food if we eat it over and over. This is why a food suddenly disappears. The good news is another food often appears, usually one that is similar to the disappearing food. That way, your brain is satisfied, and humans continue to survive!

Now that you have an idea about your own sensory differences with foods, let's talk about how you can manage them one sense at a time.

1. Managing sensory differences to the look of foods

Have a look at Diagram 3.1 which shows two boxes of oven chips.[1] Can you spot the difference?

Diagram 3.1: Packaging changes

---

1   Chips in the UK are potatoes cut into sticks and fried. In the USA, they are called 'French fries' or just 'fries'.

I knew you'd spot it; the one on the right has a sticker saying 20 per cent off. For many people, this wouldn't matter, but if you are extra sensitive to the way foods look, then a change to the packaging often means you won't eat the food inside. This is because the packaging of the food helps you trust that the food inside is your usual safe food. Unfortunately, some manufacturers change the recipe of the food at the same time as changing the packaging, which is really annoying! Some people are also sensitive to the texture of the food packaging and become anxious when this changes too. We'll cover texture sensitivity a little later in this chapter.

Other signs that you are extra sensitive to the appearance of foods are:

   ★ You eat foods that all look very similar (e.g. several types of crisp[2]).

   ★ You refuse foods that look different from normal (e.g. a black mark on a crisp).

   ★ You only eat one example of a food (e.g. one flavour of crisp).

   ★ You only eat one brand of crisp (e.g. ones from the same manufacturer).

Refusing foods that look different from usual is part of the neophobia response we learnt about in Chapter 1, where even a small change to a food or packaging means the food

---

2   Crisps in the UK are potatoes cut into very thin slices, fried and often salted or flavoured. In the USA, they are called 'potato chips' or just 'chips'.

appears as new. If you are extra sensitive to how things look, then you'll be an expert in spotting the tiniest of differences.

We met Maryam in Chapter 1; here is more of her story.

Maryam only ate salt and vinegar crisps from one brand in a blue packet. The manufacturer changed the colour of the packet to green. Now Maryam couldn't trust that the crisps inside were the same. She looked in many shops for the old packet but couldn't find any. Maryam stopped eating crisps.

Unfortunately, because Maryam stopped eating her crisps, this meant her number of safe foods reduced. Sometimes, losing a food in this way causes weight loss; that's why being able to manage changes to the look of a food is really important.

One way of Maryam overcoming this is called 'desensitisation'. This is a step-by-step way of getting used to how different examples of a food look, such as different types of chip. Simply looking at different examples of a food will help Maryam's brain to be less sensitive to the look of those foods. This means she can still eat a food even when it looks different from usual. It also means it will be easier for her to try a new example of that food that might look a little different from usual. Fortunately, after a little bit of work, Maryam was able to accept the new packaging of her favourite crisps and was even able to buy ones from a different manufacturer!

Diagram 3.2 shows some examples of different types of chips. We are now going to use this to help you desensitise to chips using Worksheet 3.2.

Diagram 3.2: Different chips

Chapter 3 Worksheet 3.2: Desensitising to Chips

Look at the examples of chips shown in Diagram 3.2. Some are from a chip shop or fast-food restaurant and some are the ones you cook at home.

Hint: If you feel disgusted by chips, skip this worksheet for now.

Now, answer these questions:

1. Which chips look best to you and why?

    ....

2. Which chips don't you like the look of and why?

    ....

3. Which ones do you think you could try?

    ....

4. Why would these chips be OK for you?

    Hint: If you already eat chips and these look similar then it will be easier.

    ....

If you were able to complete Worksheet 3.2, then well done. This shows that if you are already able to eat fries from a fast-food restaurant, perhaps you will soon be able to eat chips from the chip shop! Desensitisation can work with any food where different examples look similar to each other.

Now let's talk about managing other sensory differences.

2. Managing texture differences

Hayden hates it when there are lumps or bits in his food.

Foods with mixed textures like a stew make Alana gag and feel sick.

Ruth can't touch foods that are sticky.

Being extra sensitive to the texture of foods is often the first food issue parents notice. This is because when babies start to eat foods instead of just having milk, they may show some texture sensitivity, such as spitting out or gagging on lumpy foods (a gag is like when we are about to be sick). This is quite common as babies are still learning about foods. For some babies, these sensitivities continue, and they refuse lumpy foods or foods with bits in as they get older. The problem with refusing these foods is that a cycle develops where the child never learns to manage these trickier textures. If you are autistic or neurodivergent and have avoidant eating, then this may have happened to you. This can explain why some textures are hard for you now.

Fact Finder 3.2: My texture history

You may be interested in your own texture history. If so, you can ask your family or carers if you were sensitive to texture when you were younger. Questions you can ask them are:

1. Did I gag/spit out lumpy foods as a baby?

2. Did I refuse to eat foods with lumps or bits in?

3. Did I refuse to eat foods with a mixed texture (e.g. spaghetti bolognese)?

Then ask yourself this question:

4. Do I eat or refuse these foods now?

If the answer is yes to these questions, then you will know when your texture sensitivity started.

Remember that everyone has a unique sensory system, so let's find out which textures you do eat.

✓

Chapter 3 Worksheet 3.3: My Food Textures

Read the list of food textures and examples below.

They are in order from easiest to chew/swallow to the hardest.

Tick (✓) those textures you are able to eat and put a cross (**X**) by the ones you can't.

1. Smooth puree (e.g. stewed fruit, smooth yoghurt, custard) ☐

2. Soft mash (e.g. mashed potato/banana, dhal) ☐

3. Bite and dissolve (e.g. puff crisps, wafer biscuits) ☐

4. Bite and melt (e.g. chocolate buttons) ☐

5. Bite and soft chew (e.g. soft peeled fruit, pasta, cake) ☐

6. Bite and splinter (e.g. breadsticks, crackers, crisps) ☐

7. Bite and lump (e.g. raw apple/carrot, crusty bread) ☐

Write here which textures you like the best:

. . . .

Understanding which textures are OK for you now really helps when it comes to choosing a new food. We'll learn how to choose a new food in Chapter 5. It's also a good idea to tell other people, particularly anyone who is cooking or preparing food for you, which textures are OK for you and which ones are not. For example, you might like potatoes when they are fried like chips but may hate them when they are mashed like mashed potato.

Let's find out how you can desensitise your mouth to help you eat different textures.

The mouth (along with our fingertips) is one of the most sensitive parts of our body. In order to desensitise your mouth, you should start with the textures you are already able to eat and only move to the next stage when you are ready. For example, if you can only cope with smooth foods, then the next stage to try is bite and dissolve foods. Work through the stages at your own pace until you reach the hardest textures. Desensitising other parts of the body first, such as your hands, can also help.

Desensitising activities

Desensitising activities work best when they are done as often as you can; the more you do them, the easier it will be. Remember to always go at your own pace.

To desensitise your hands:

1. Do some craft work (e.g. sticking/finger painting).

2. Touch different food textures; start with dry (e.g. dry pasta) then sticky (e.g. jelly).

3. Do some baking or cooking.

4. Make your own slime or gloop.

5. Squeeze a stress ball or fidget toy.

6. Do chores that use your hands (e.g. washing the car, vacuuming).

To desensitise your face:

1. Do some face painting; have fun doing it with a friend.

2. Play with putting different textures on your lips (e.g. 'lipstick yoghurt'!).

3. Massage your face using fingers to press in small circles on your cheeks or forehead.

    Hint: If face massage is too hard, massage other body parts first (e.g. arms).

To desensitise your mouth:

1. Massage your gums and inside of cheeks with a finger or a soft toothbrush.

    Hint: If this is too hard, start with your lips.

2. Use an electric toothbrush to massage the inside of your mouth.

3. Suck an ice cube or ice lolly.

4. Chew on a safe object (e.g. a chewy buddy).

    Hint: Ask an adult to help you buy one to make sure it is safe.

Let's talk now about managing smell and taste differences.

3. Managing smell and taste differences

Read Raj's story:

Raj couldn't stand the smells of other people's food; in fact, they made him feel sick. At college, Raj did work experience in the college café. After three months, Raj was able to sit with his friends and eat in the café.

How was Raj able to go from not being able to cope with smells to sitting with his friends in the café? The answer is natural desensitisation. Just by working in the café, Raj got slowly used to the different food smells which enabled him to be more comfortable with smells and eventually to be able to eat in the café.

Other examples of natural desensitisation activities for smell include:

* ★ shopping in the supermarket

* ★ preparing and cooking food – you don't have to eat it, just make it

* ★ sitting near other people who are eating.

Natural desensitisation gets your senses used to new experiences. Doing this as part of an activity you enjoy will help you cope with any anxiety.

Have you ever had a bad cold with a blocked-up nose and

found that you couldn't taste anything? That's because a lot of what we taste is actually smell. That means desensitising to smell also helps us cope with new tastes.

Fact Finder 3.3: The science of smell and taste

Smells enter the nose as airborne molecules, and then our brains identify what the smell is. Scientists think we can identify millions of different smells!

Taste molecules are released when we chew foods, and these are identified by taste buds on the tongue. Scientists have found there are five types of taste: sweet, salt, sour, bitter and umami (savoury). Taste molecules are also picked up by our noses, and it is the combination of taste and smell that tells us what we are eating.

As there is no gravity in space, taste and smell molecules can't be picked up, so astronauts can't tell what they are eating!

The secret to success with all desensitisation activities is to go at your own pace but to challenge yourself a little bit more each time without becoming anxious or overloaded. We'll talk about coping with sensory overload in Chapter 6.

4. Managing appetite differences

In Chapter 1, we learnt that differences in recognising appetite are common in autistic and neurodivergent people. This is because of interoception differences – our sense of what is happening inside our bodies.

Appetite is the brain signal that makes sure we eat enough and don't starve, and that we don't overeat and become overweight. Another part of appetite is how much we enjoy eating.

The Wonka gum

Many people with avoidant eating say they don't enjoy eating. Some young people have told me they wish there was a pill that could replace eating!

This reminded me of the character Violet in Roald Dahl's book 'Charlie and the Chocolate Factory' (2016). Violet is obsessed with chewing gum and eats the gum Willy Wonka has invented that replaces a three-course meal. Of course, no good comes to Violet, and she turns into one of the replacement foods – a giant blueberry!

That makes me think it is far better to help people with avoidant eating learn to enjoy at least some foods!

How do you know you have problems recognising appetite? Here are some signs:

* Not eating for a long time and then eating a lot in one meal.

   Hint: This is the brain making up for lost calories.[3]

* Eating small amounts throughout the day instead of meals.

   Hint: This is called 'grazing'.

* Feeling hungry all the time and always eating.

   Hint: This is overeating and it can mean becoming overweight.

* Feeling 'hangry' – this is feeling angry or irritable because you are hungry.

   Hint: Try to notice when this happens (e.g. close to mealtimes).

* Being tired and having headaches are also signs that you actually might be hungry.

   Hint: Try to notice when these happen (e.g. close to mealtimes).

---

3   Kilocalories (kcals) are a measure of how much energy different foods contain.

> ## Top Tip: Calories, calories, calories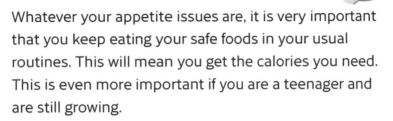
>
> Whatever your appetite issues are, it is very important that you keep eating your safe foods in your usual routines. This will mean you get the calories you need. This is even more important if you are a teenager and are still growing.

The good news is that it is possible to train the brain to recognise feelings of hunger or fullness. Try the following:

★ Eat something every two to three hours; this helps your brain learn to expect food.

★ Eat six times a day: breakfast, mid-morning, lunch, mid-afternoon, teatime/dinner, before bed.

★ Eat at the same time each day; this keeps your energy levels stable.

★ Remind yourself it's time to eat by setting an alarm.

★ Always have some safe foods with you so you can eat regularly.

Worksheet 3.4 will help you learn to spot the signs of hunger; you can also use it to spot the signs of being full.

Chapter 3 Worksheet 3.4: The Appetite Drone

Do this exercise about 15 minutes before eating.

Hint: If you are doing it to recognise feelings of fullness, do it 15 minutes after eating.

Follow the steps below:

1. Sit somewhere quiet without any distractions.

2. Breathe in and out slowly for 3 breaths.

3. Now imagine you are controlling a drone and fly it over your body.

4. What feelings does it pick up in your body and where? Write them here:

   . . . .

5. Hover it above your stomach. What feelings does it pick up? Write them here:

   . . . .

6. Do you notice signs of hunger (e.g. an emptiness, growling or gurgling)?

   . . . .

7. Do you notice signs of fullness (e.g. your stomach feeling full like a balloon)?

   . . . .

8. Now fly the drone away and sit up slowly; this exercise can make you sleepy.

What did you notice when you flew the drone over your stomach? Hopefully, the drone helped you notice signs of hunger or fullness. Practising this exercise regularly can help you learn what hunger and feeling full feel like in your body. It can also help you notice other feelings, such as tiredness or stress. This is important because when we are stressed, our appetite can change. In fact, many autistic or neurodivergent people eat even less than usual when stressed, and they may lose weight, become ill or not have enough energy for their usual activities. If this happens to you, it is really important you try to eat as many of your safe foods as you can and speak to a trusted adult to get some more support.

We'll talk more about managing anxiety around foods in the next chapter.

Top Tip: HCPM foods

If you are stressed and you are eating less than usual, then choose foods that are 'high calorie per mouthful' (HCPM) – for example, chocolate, biscuits or a cereal bar. These foods have quite a lot of calories in each mouthful, so you don't have to eat a lot to get the energy you need. They are also useful for when you don't have much time to eat, such as at school or college.

Now we've got to the end of Chapter 3, what have we learnt?

Summary of Chapter 3

✓ How sensory differences cause eating issues and are part of avoidant eating.

✓ More about your own sensory differences and how they impact on your eating.

✓ How to desensitise to the appearance of foods, including the packaging.

✓ How to manage texture sensitivity by desensitising your hands, face and mouth.

✓ Why natural desensitisation (e.g. cooking) can help you cope with smells and tastes.

✓ How to train your brain to recognise appetite more easily.

✓ How to recognise how your body feels inside when you are hungry or full.

✓ Why continuing to eat your safe foods during stress and anxiety is really important.

Chapter 4

Managing My Anxiety about Food and Eating

Reminder of what we learnt in Chapter 3:

- ★ How sensory differences cause eating issues and are part of avoidant eating.

- ★ More about your own sensory differences and how they impact on your eating.

- ★ How to desensitise to the appearance of foods, including the packaging.

- ★ How to manage texture sensitivity by desensitising your hands, face and mouth.

- ★ Why natural desensitisation (e.g. cooking) can help you cope with smells and tastes.

- ★ How to train your brain to recognise appetite more easily.

- ★ How to recognise how your body feels inside when you are hungry or full.

- ★ Why continuing to eat your safe foods during stress and anxiety is really important.

Introduction

In Year 3 we had a new head teacher who was big on healthy eating. I was terrified that the new rules would mean I'd have to go hungry at school! (Rachel)

I'm actually scared of food. Sometimes I see my friends eating things and I think I'd like to try them, but when I do, I'm just too anxious. I'd really like to be able to go out with my friends and eat something but I just can't. (Maryam)

If, like Rachel or Maryam you are anxious, scared or stressed around food, then this chapter will be an important one for you. Anxiety plays a big role in causing problems with food and in keeping those problems from going away. Chapter 4 aims to teach you more about the role of anxiety in eating and enable you to overcome it.

In this chapter you will discover:

★ what anxiety is, and the science behind it

★ what situations or 'triggers' make you anxious

★ what happens to our bodies and brains when we are anxious

★ why anxiety is bad for eating

★ how anxious thoughts, feelings, body changes and behaviour are all connected

* how to manage anxious thoughts, feelings and body changes

* how relaxation can reduce your anxiety around foods and eating

* why families get anxious about their teenager's eating and how you can help.

What is anxiety?

Anxiety is a feeling of worry, fear or nervousness. It often happens when things are uncertain or when you don't know what is going to happen next. This can cause your body and brain to experience stress. Everybody feels stress from time to time, and feeling anxious is part of being human. Common situations that can cause stress include:

* taking an exam or test

* having a job interview

* dealing with a big change such as moving house

* having problems in a relationship or with a friend.

Many autistic and neurodivergent people experience more stress than other people and feel anxious more often. This is because it can be harder to cope with change or manage relationships, for example.

Worksheet 4.1 will help you to learn what situations or 'triggers' cause you stress or anxiety. This is useful, as it is the first step to managing them.

Chapter 4 Worksheet 4.1: My Anxiety Triggers

Make a list of all the triggers you can think of that make you anxious.

Hint: Think about situations you usually don't like or avoid.

Write them here and put a star (*****) by the ones that cause you the most anxiety.

1. ....

2. ....

3. ....

4. ....

5. ....

6. ....

7. ....

8. ....

Knowing what triggers your anxiety is helpful in knowing
how to manage it and in planning the changes you want to
make to your eating. Let's look now at how you can tell that
you are anxious, worried or scared. Learning what happens
to our bodies when we are anxious is a good place to begin.

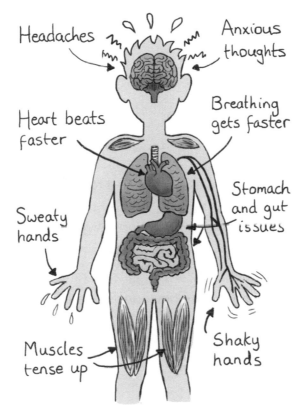

Diagram 4.1: Anxiety and the body

Diagram 4.1 shows what happens to our body when we get
anxious. This includes:

★ Our heart beats faster.

★ Our muscles get tight and tense up.

★ Our breathing becomes faster.

★ We may need to go to the toilet more often.

Do any of these happen to you? Let's find out why.

Imagine you are back thousands of years ago when humans hunted and gathered their food. You are out hunting when suddenly you see danger: a sabre-toothed tiger is coming towards you looking for its next meal! What do you do? Your choices are:

★ Pick up a rock or spear and fight the tiger.

★ Run away from the tiger.

★ Stay very still and hide from the tiger.

Whatever choice you make, you need to be ready for action in order to avoid being eaten. Like animals, humans have evolved ways to protect ourselves from danger. When we are stressed or afraid, our brain releases chemicals called 'hormones' into our body, which gets us ready to deal with the stressful situation. The hormones cause body changes such as:

★ Our muscles become tense and ready for action so we can 'fight'.

★ Our hearts beat faster to send more blood to our muscles to help us run or take 'flight'.

★ Our brains focus on our environment so we can react such as staying still or 'freeze'.

These changes are known as the 'fight, flight, freeze' response, which happens automatically when there is a threat or something to be scared of. Once the stress has gone, our bodies release other hormones to help us relax and feel calmer.

Today there are no sabre-toothed tigers, but our brains and bodies still react in the same way whenever we are stressed or anxious. Later in the chapter, we will look at ideas for relaxing your brain and body, even in stressful situations, to help you manage them.

Let's look now at how anxiety affects eating.

Anxiety and eating

Quite simply, anxiety is bad for eating. Let's see why.

* When we are anxious, our mouths go dry and we need to go to the toilet more. These body changes are designed to get us ready for action. However, it is also hard to eat with a dry mouth or if you need to go to the toilet. That's why it's hard to eat when you are stressed.

* The 'fight, flight, freeze' response makes our brains more aware of what is going on around us. This means our brains notice changes to foods even more than normal, neophobia gets worse, and we may stop eating even our safe foods.

* Anxiety causes our sensory systems to become more sensitive to the look, feel, smell and taste of foods. This may mean even our safe foods are not OK.

* Eating and mealtimes are stressful for autistic and neurodivergent people, and because these happen several times a day, they are always anxious. This means the 'fight, flight, freeze' response never goes away.

It is easy to see why anxiety and stress stop you from eating, particularly if you are autistic or neurodivergent. Let's talk now about how to manage your anxiety by first understanding how anxious thoughts, feelings, body changes and behaviour are all connected.

Read Raj's story.

 Raj has been invited to a party but is worried that the food smells will make him be sick and that he will be embarrassed. Raj's heart begins to beat faster, so he messages the host of the party to tell them he can't go.

Does Raj's story sound familiar? If so, then you might already know that anxiety doesn't just cause changes to our bodies, but it also changes how we think, feel and behave.

Chapter 4 Worksheet 4.2: Thought, Feeling, Body or Behaviour?

Read Raj's story again. This time, write in the brackets whether it is a **thought**, **feeling**, **body change** or **behaviour** that Raj is experiencing.

Hint: You need to use all 4 once.

Raj has been invited to a party but is worried that the food smells will make him be sick (...............................) and that he will be embarrassed (...............................). Raj's heart begins to beat faster (...............................), so he messages the host of the party to tell them he can't go (...............................).

Hopefully, you managed to identify Raj's thoughts (worries about being sick), feelings (embarrassment), body changes (heart beating fast) and behaviour (not going to the party).

Raj's story tells us that anxiety is a combination of thoughts, feelings, body changes and behaviour, all of which are connected and happen as part of a cycle.

This is called the Anxiety 'Hot Cross Bun'.

Fact Finder 4.1: The Anxiety Hot Cross Bun

A hot cross bun is a bakery item usually sold at Easter, and the top is marked with a cross. What does this have to do with anxiety? In the 1970s, Professor Aaron Beck invented a new therapy for anxiety and depression called Cognitive Behaviour Therapy or 'CBT' (Beck et al., 1979). CBT teaches that thoughts, feelings, body changes and behaviour are all connected; this is the 'Hot Cross Bun' shown in Diagram 4.2.

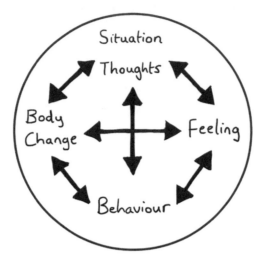

Diagram 4.2: The Anxiety Hot Cross Bun

Remember Raj? He was relieved that he didn't go to the party, but the next time he was invited, the same thing happened and soon he was avoiding all social occasions. When anxiety is uncontrolled, an unhelpful cycle (sometimes called a 'vicious cycle') can quickly develop. CBT aims to stop the cycle by tackling anxious thoughts, feelings, body changes and behaviour step by step.

Managing the Hot Cross Bun

So, if you are like Raj, caught in a vicious cycle of anxiety, particularly around food, let's enable you to manage all aspects of the Hot Cross Bun.

Let's see how Raj challenged his anxious thoughts. This is similar to Worksheet 2.2 in Chapter 2 where you learnt to challenge your worries about change.

There are three steps for Raj in challenging his anxious thoughts:

1. For Raj to *identify* the anxious thought:

   e.g. *I'm worried the food smells will make me sick.*

2. For Raj to find *evidence* to *challenge* the anxious thought:

   e.g. *Even though I feel sick, I've not actually been sick.*

3. For Raj to *replace* the anxious thought with a *positive* one:

   e.g. *So it's unlikely I'll be sick, and I may even be able to try it!*

Now, use Worksheet 4.3 to have a go at challenging your own anxious thoughts.

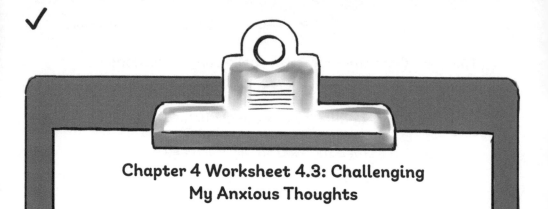

Chapter 4 Worksheet 4.3: Challenging My Anxious Thoughts

Imagine you are a lawyer in court arguing the case against the thought.

Follow the 3 steps below and fill in the thought bubbles.

1. Identify the anxious thought:

2. Find evidence to challenge the anxious thought:

3. Replace the anxious thought with a positive one:

Do this every time you want to challenge an anxious thought about your eating.

The Hot Cross Bun means anxious thoughts, feelings, body changes and behaviour are all connected. This helps, because challenging anxious thoughts will also help with managing anxious feelings. Sometimes autistic or neurodivergent teenagers find it difficult to recognise their feelings. This is because of differences in interoception or the way we recognise what is happening inside our bodies. The good news is that this gets easier as you get older and as you have more experience with different feelings.

Worksheet 4.4 will help you work out some of your feelings about food and eating.

Chapter 4 Worksheet 4.4: My Anxious Feelings

Here are some of the feelings other young people have about their eating:

Embarrassed

Fed up

Stressed

Frustrated

Use the blank bubbles to add your own feelings.

Hint: Think about the times when eating is hard for you.

I know these feelings might seem negative now; this is because we are only halfway through the book and you are still learning how you can change your eating. Chapters 5 and 7 contain more examples of where young people have successfully changed their eating and how this made them feel; hopefully, this will empower you and help you feel positive!

I have spent a lot of my career as a psychologist helping young people who have avoidant eating. One of the best ways I have found for managing anxiety is learning to relax.

Relaxation manages anxious thoughts, feelings and body changes, so it is an excellent all-round method for reducing the 'fight, flight, freeze' response.

There are three methods of relaxation:

- ★ Deep breathing – this slows the heart rate, calms the body and can be used anywhere.

- ★ Muscle relaxation – this helps the whole body feel less tense.

- ★ Visualisation – this uses imagination to 'switch off' anxious thoughts.

Remember, everyone is different, so it is a good idea to try all three methods. It is also a good idea to record your relaxation levels before and after you have tried them so you can see which method works best for you. If you are autistic or neurodivergent, a visual scale is best. There is a Relaxation Rating Scale in Appendix 1 that you can copy and use as many times as you like.

Let's start with learning to breathe deeply; Worksheet 4.5 will help you.

Chapter 4 Worksheet 4.5: Deep Breathing

1. Find a quiet place and sit upright; shut your eyes if you want to.

2. Place one hand on your chest and the other on your stomach.

3. Breathe in through your nose and count to 3; notice how your stomach rises up.

   Hint: This is because your lungs are full of air and this pushes on your stomach.

4. Breathe out and count to 3; notice how your stomach goes down.

   Hint: This is because your lungs are emptying the air and your stomach relaxes.

5. Repeat 10 times.

6. Use the Relaxation Rating Scale in Appendix 1 to rate how relaxed you feel.

   Hint: To know if this method has worked for you, rate yourself before too.

Learning to breathe deeply is very useful for reducing anxiety about foods and mealtimes. That's because it can be used anywhere and no one will notice you were using it. It can also be an emergency technique in a tricky situation, as even two or three deep breaths will calm you down. Chapter 5 will explain how taking some deep breaths before trying a food for the first time also makes it easier to try it.

Remember our story earlier about the sabre-toothed tiger? Then you'll remember that the 'fight, flight, freeze' response is all about getting ready for action. One way the body gets ready for action is that the muscles in our bodies become tense.

Worksheet 4.6 will help you learn to relax your muscles in order to reduce anxiety.

Chapter 4 Worksheet 4.6: Relaxing My Body

This exercise takes about 5 minutes.

Hint: Go at your own pace and tense the muscles gently; not so hard that they hurt.

1. Find a quiet place to sit comfortably or lie down.

2. Take 10 deep breaths (see Worksheet 4.5: Deep Breathing).

3. Squeeze your hands into fists and tense for 3 seconds, then release.

4. Bend your arms and touch your shoulders and tense for 3 seconds, then release.

5. Hunch your shoulders up to your ears and tense for 3 seconds, then release.

6. Shut your eyes tightly and tense for 3 seconds, then release.

7. Tense the muscles in your stomach for 3 seconds, then release.

8. Point your toes downward and tense for 3 seconds, then release.

9. Point your toes upward and tense for 3 seconds, then release.

10. Use the Relaxation Rating Scale in Appendix 1 to rate how relaxed you feel.

    Hint: To know if this method has worked for you, rate yourself before too.

Our last relaxation method is visualisation or imagining being in a calm and relaxing place. This is a great technique to 'switch off' an anxious brain.

Worksheet 4.7 will help you have a go.

Chapter 4 Worksheet 4.7: Relaxing My Brain

This exercise takes about 10 minutes. Find a quiet place to sit comfortably or lie down. Use the guide below to imagine being in a beautiful and peaceful place.

Hint: Don't pick somewhere too exciting; picking a place you have been to (e.g. on holiday) can make it easier.

It works best if you close your eyes.

Follow these steps:

1. Take 10 deep breaths (see Worksheet 4.5: Deep Breathing).
2. Imagine a staircase with 10 steps. Walk down the staircase and count down from 10.
3. At the bottom is a door. Go through the door; you are standing in a beautiful place.
4. Imagine what this place looks and sounds like now.
5. You feel very safe and very relaxed in this beautiful place.
6. Walk and explore the beautiful place; imagine what you see, hear, touch and smell.
7. All of these make you feel safe and very relaxed here.
8. Spend some time now in this beautiful place doing whatever you like.
9. Now walk back to the door and climb the stairs; count up to 10 as you go.
10. Use the Relaxation Rating Scale in Appendix 1 to rate how relaxed you feel.

    Hint: To know if this method has worked for you, rate yourself before too.

Once you have picked a relaxing place, this exercise can be done as many times as you like. Many people find it helps them switch off at night, so they sleep better. With all relaxation methods, practice is the key; the more you do them, the easier it will be for you.

Why do families get anxious about eating?

I know you have experience of this! If there is one section of this book that you might want to show to an adult, then it is this one. This is because I want to talk about how their anxiety can affect you.

Did you know that anxiety is catching? We can pick it up from each other, especially our friends and family. Unfortunately, this only makes everyone's anxiety much worse.

Read Taylor's story.

Taylor is autistic and has ARFID. Sometimes they don't eat for a long time, which makes their mum anxious that Taylor will lose weight or become ill, so Taylor's mum nags them to eat more. This makes Taylor anxious and so they eat even less. This makes Taylor's mum even more anxious.

Both Taylor and their mum are caught in a vicious cycle of each other's anxiety. It is really common for unhelpful cycles like this to develop, but it is important you know that it isn't anyone's fault. It just means that families and teenagers both need to understand about avoidant eating. This reduces everyone's anxiety.

Here are some of the worries parents have about their teenager's eating:

They'll get ill and have to go to hospital.

They won't have the energy to go to school.

What will I do if I can't find their safe foods?

People will think I'm a terrible parent.

Here are what parents sometimes do when they are worried about your eating:

★ Nag or pressure you to eat more.

★ Try to get you to eat other, perhaps 'healthier' foods, instead of your safe ones.

★ Hide another food or a vitamin and mineral supplement in your safe food.

★ Bribe or reward you to try a different food.

★ Put your safe food in old packaging when the packaging changes.

★ Make you sit at the table until you've eaten everything.

Unfortunately, research tells us that these strategies don't work. In fact, they just cause more anxiety for teenagers, which means they eat less, not more! This in turn causes parents to worry more, and so the vicious cycle continues.

The pushy waiter

Imagine you are at a restaurant and your favourite meal arrives. The waiter stands behind you, and each time you have a mouthful of food, he says, 'Have another one.' This gets more and more irritating until, in the end, you stop eating altogether. That's what nagging or pressure to eat feels like! Now imagine that the waiter won't let you leave the table until you have finished all your meal, or that he had hidden something in your food. I bet at this point you'll be ready to run out of the restaurant!

So what can Taylor and their mum do differently?

Here are my top 3 family and teenager guidelines to reduce everyone's anxiety:

What families can do:	What teenagers can do:
Take time to understand.	Show them this book to explain.
Always allow safe foods.	Keep eating your safe foods.
Don't pressure or nag.	Tell your family how you feel.

Learning about avoidant eating helped Taylor's mum understand what Taylor needed. Being listened to and explaining their feelings helped Taylor feel supported. This way, everyone understands each other and can work together to help teens with avoidant eating.

So now we've got to the end of Chapter 4, what have we learnt?

Summary of Chapter 4

✓ What anxiety is and the science behind it.

✓ What triggers your own anxiety.

✓ What happens to our bodies and brains in the 'fight, flight, freeze' response.

✓ Why anxiety is bad for eating.

✓ How anxious thoughts, feelings, body changes and behaviour are all connected.

✓ Why the Hot Cross Bun can be helpful in managing anxiety.

✓ How to challenge anxious thoughts about food and eating.

✓ How to recognise anxious feelings about food and eating.

✓ How relaxation reduces anxiety around foods and eating.

✓ Why parents and families worry about eating and how teenagers can help them.

Chapter 5

How to Try a New Food

Reminder of what we learnt in Chapter 4:

★ What anxiety is and the science behind it.

★ What triggers your own anxiety.

★ What happens to our bodies and brains in the 'fight, flight, freeze' response.

★ Why anxiety is bad for eating.

★ How anxious thoughts, feelings, body changes and behaviour are all connected.

★ Why the Hot Cross Bun can be helpful in managing anxiety.

★ How to challenge anxious thoughts about food and eating.

★ How to recognise anxious feelings about food and eating.

★ How relaxation reduces anxiety around foods and eating.

★ Why parents and families worry about eating and how teenagers can help them.

Introduction

I wouldn't want to try new foods because they might make me sick, so we thought about what I already liked, and tried to gradually extend it. (Rachel)

If, like Rachel, you're fed up with the foods you eat but are still anxious about trying anything new, then this chapter is for you. Remember neophobia from Chapter 1? Many autistic and neurodivergent teenagers find trying new foods really difficult because neophobia doesn't go away easily for them. Add to this the sensory differences we explored in Chapter 3 and the anxiety about eating we looked at in Chapter 4, and it's no surprise that trying a new and unfamiliar food can be a real challenge.

The good news is that as you become a teenager, overcoming these challenges becomes easier. This is because motivation to change and your ability to cope with anxiety and sensory differences increase. The other good news is that by reading this book, you have already learnt most of the techniques you will need to try a new food successfully. Chapter 5 aims to bring these together to enable you to choose and try a new food for the first time.

In this chapter you will discover:

★ what doesn't work when trying a new food

★ how to know you are ready to start

★ how to choose a new food to try

★ how to prepare for trying it (a reminder of desensitising and reducing anxiety)

★ how to set up and complete a 'taste trial'

★ how to find out whether you like the new food or not

★ why it can be easier to try a new food in a new place

★ why you should celebrate every small win.

What doesn't work

Warning: We are smarter than you think! Tricking a teenager with a new food, disguised in the packaging of their trusted brands, does not work; it usually makes things worse. (Rachel)

Again, it might sound strange to start a chapter on trying a new food with what not to do, but, as Rachel says, some things make avoidant eating worse. Here are some of the things that don't work and why:

★ Pressure to eat (e.g. nagging or forcing) – this just makes you more anxious.

★ Bribes or rewards – these don't help if you are anxious or the food is disgusting.

★ Hiding a new food in a safe food – this risks contamination.

★ Putting a new food on your plate at meals – this risks contamination.

★ Sitting in front of a new food – this risks making you anxious.

★ Waiting until you are hungry – if you don't recognise appetite, you won't feel hungry.

So make sure you – or anyone else who is supporting you – don't do any of these!

How do I know I'm ready to start?

Chapter 2 explored how to know if you are ready to make changes to your eating. Let's remind ourselves how you can check if you are ready to try a new food for the first time.

We met Stephan in Chapter 1; read more of his story.

Stephan noticed that he didn't mind any more that the packaging of his crisps sometimes changed. He's even been able to eat a different brand. Stephan had got bored of some of his foods and was interested in the foods his friends were eating at school.

Stephan's story contains signs that he might be ready to try a new food. These are:

★ accepting changes to a safe food (e.g. the packaging or brand)

★ getting bored of safe foods – this means being ready for something new

★ being interested in what friends are eating – this is an excellent motivator.

If any of these signs are true for you, then you are definitely ready to start the next stage: choosing a new food.

How to choose a new food

Your parents let you eat crisps and chocolate all the time? You're so lucky. Have you ever tried chicken tikka? (Rachel's friend)

Rachel's friend thinks she is lucky that she eats chocolate and crisps all the time, but Rachel was bored and really wanted to eat something new. Rachel's friend suggested she try chicken tikka, but Rachel didn't want to try this.

So how do we choose a new food? There are two ways to do this:

1. Choose a food that is *similar* to one you already eat (e.g. a new flavour or brand).

2. Choose a food you are *motivated* to eat (e.g. one you have a very good reason to eat).

Let's start by using Worksheet 5.1 to choose something very similar to what you already eat.

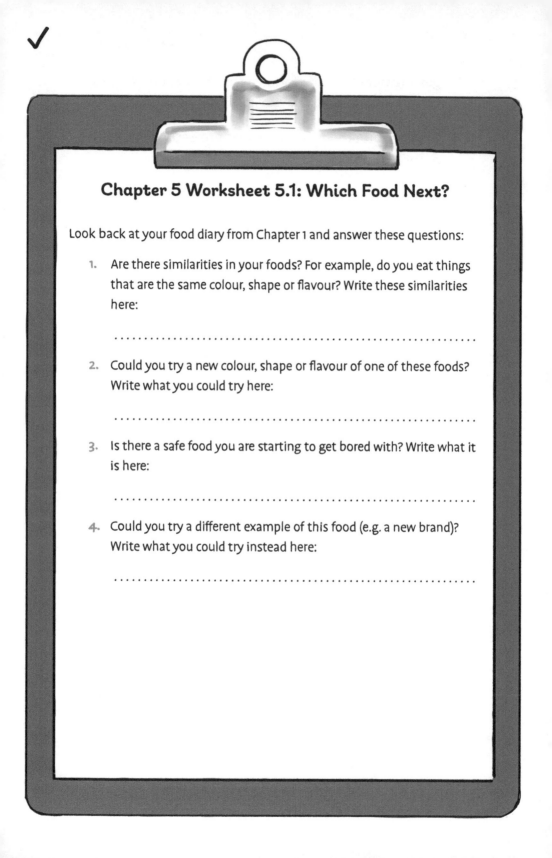

Chapter 5 Worksheet 5.1: Which Food Next?

Look back at your food diary from Chapter 1 and answer these questions:

1. Are there similarities in your foods? For example, do you eat things that are the same colour, shape or flavour? Write these similarities here:

   . . . .

2. Could you try a new colour, shape or flavour of one of these foods? Write what you could try here:

   . . . .

3. Is there a safe food you are starting to get bored with? Write what it is here:

   . . . .

4. Could you try a different example of this food (e.g. a new brand)? Write what you could try instead here:

   . . . .

For Stephan, looking at different examples of foods gave him a clue as to what could be next. He decided he would try some different types of crisp because he liked the look of the ones his friends were eating. This is similar to the desensitising to chips exercise you did in Chapter 3. A trip to the supermarket can help. Here are some ideas:

* ★ Go to a shop that sells the food you are thinking of adding (e.g. bread).

* ★ Have a look at the different examples of bread.

* ★ Ask yourself which ones are similar to the one you already eat.

* ★ If there's one that looks OK, buy it and make a plan for trying it.

Top Tip: Similar foods

Choosing a food that is similar to one you already like is the easiest way to try a new food for the first time. That's because it is already familiar and will be easy for your brain to get used to.

Starting with a very similar food is not only the easiest way to begin, but it has other benefits too. These include:

* ★ Your brain gets less bored and so you don't stop eating some of your safe foods.

* ★ You have more choice, especially if you can't get your safe food.

★ Your brain becomes more flexible, so it is easier to try a different food next time.

★ Your confidence in being able to make changes increases.

Health and safety reminder

Remember, if you have any food sensitivities, allergies or intolerances, it is extremely important that any new food you pick for trying is safe for you. If you are unsure, speak to a health professional before going any further with this chapter.

The second method of choosing a new food is to pick one you are very motivated to eat. In Chapter 2, we looked at some of the motivators other autistic and neurodivergent teenagers have for making a change to their eating. These included wanting to eat something with friends or on holiday.

Look back at Worksheet 2.4 as a reminder of what your motivators are and then use Worksheet 5.2 to identify some possible new foods you could try and why.

Chapter 5 Worksheet 5.2: New Foods I Could Try and Why

Try to think of 3 new foods you would like to try; write them here:

Food 1: . . . .

Food 2: . . . .

Food 3: . . . .

Now think of a reason why you are motivated to try each food and write them here:

Reason for food 1: . . . .

Reason for food 2: . . . .

Reason for food 3: . . . .

Which of these 3 foods could you try first? Write it here:

. . . .

Do you remember Dan from Chapter 2? He wanted to eat peanuts, but his mum chose a food that was disgusting to him instead. The most important thing when choosing a new food is that it must be your choice and not someone else's. If Rachel had wanted to try chicken tikka, then this might have been a helpful suggestion from her friend; Rachel didn't, so it wasn't helpful. Rachel decided to try a food that she was motivated to eat – toast. We'll hear more about how she achieved this a little later in this chapter.

Top Tip: Take your time

I have noticed that young people have more success in trying a new food for the first time if they have really thought about which food to try and why. So spend as much time as you need to on deciding which food could be right for you. That way, you are more likely to be able to try and like it.

Preparing to try the food

Once you have chosen the food you would like to try, the next step is to desensitise to that food as much as possible. This is easier if you are going to try a food that is similar to one you already eat, such as a new brand, shape or flavour. If it is a totally new and different food, then you may need to spend a bit more time on this step.

Chapter 3 explained how to desensitise to different foods; you may want to look back at that chapter now. Here is a reminder:

★ Sit next to someone eating the food; ask them what it is like and why they like it.

★ Go to a shop or supermarket and look at the different examples of the food.

★ Prepare and cook the food; this is just desensitisation – you don't have to eat it yet.

★ Explore the food – for example, touch and smell it.

Hint: The smell tells you how it might taste.

You are also likely at this point to be feeling anxious, as tasting the food for the first time is coming up. One way to deal with your anxiety is to make a plan for what you will do if something unexpected happens. Here are some ideas you could include:

★ It is easier to try a new food without an audience, so plan a time you can be alone.

Hint: If you are worried you might have a reaction to a new food then make sure you have an adult with you when you try it.

★ Do the deep breathing exercise from Chapter 4 immediately before trying the food.

★ Challenge anxious thoughts using the methods from Chapter 4.

★ Many people worry they will be sick; if this is you, have a bowl ready just in case.

Another way to manage anxiety about trying a new food is to adapt the visualisation exercise from Chapter 4 to include a section on food. The idea is that if you can imagine trying a new food whilst relaxed, it will be easier for you to do so in the 'real' world:

Worksheet 5.3 will help you do this.

Chapter 5 Worksheet 5.3: Imagining Eating a New Food

The relaxation exercise below contains a section on eating with positive suggestions for new behaviour, such as being able to eat a new food. Add your safe foods and the new food that you want to try in the blank spaces.

Now have a go.

1. Take 10 deep breaths (see Worksheet 4.5: Deep Breathing).

2. Imagine a staircase with 10 steps. Walk down the staircase and count down from 10.

3. At the bottom is a door. Go through; you are standing in a beautiful place.

4. Walk and explore the beautiful place; imagine what you see, hear, touch and smell.

5. You find a table with your safe foods – e.g. ....
   and a new food – e.g. ....

6. You feel hungry, so you eat some of your safe foods and then try the new food.

7. You feel safe and relaxed and in control of what you are eating.

8. You feel proud you tried the new food and confident you'll be able to do this again.

9. Now walk back to the door and climb the stairs; count up to 10 as you go.

10. Use the Relaxation Rating Scale in Appendix 1 to rate how relaxed you feel.

    Hint: To know if this method has worked for you, rate yourself before too.

You can take this relaxation exercise and change whatever you like. In fact, it's a good idea if you make it personal to you. If you are autistic or neurodivergent and find imagination difficult, here are some ideas to get you started:

* ★ Imagine a real place such as somewhere you've been on holiday.

* ★ Use visual reminders – for example, photographs or drawings of the place.

* ★ Examples of possible relaxing places include beaches, mountains, forests, lakes.

* ★ Avoid imagining scenes from video games; these are generally not relaxing!

So you've decided you are ready; you've chosen a new food and spent some time desensitising to it and reducing your anxiety. Let's talk now about how you actually try it!

How to set up and complete a taste trial

Trying a new food for the first time can be scary. A 'taste trial' is an experiment to see if you like the food or not. Just like the experiments you may do at school or college, there are rules and a method to follow. These will help you step by step.

Here are the rules:

* ★ Continue to eat your safe foods; this will keep you as healthy as possible.

* ★ Don't do a taste trial when there is extra stress; the

section 'When not to make changes' at the beginning of Chapter 2 explains this more.

★ Don't do a taste trial at your usual mealtimes; this just adds extra pressure.

Here is the method:

1. Set aside a regular time to do the taste trial (e.g. every day after school).

2. Do some relaxation immediately before trying the food.

3. Then try a small amount of the new food (e.g. a piece the size of a coin).

4. Use the Taste Trial Rating Scale in Appendix 1 to rate what you think of the food.

   Hint: If the rating is five or more on your first try, this is good. If the rating is three or lower, this is not so good; you may need to try a different food.

5. Record the date on a timetable or calendar each time you try the food.

6. Give yourself a reward for having a go and be proud that you tried it.

7. Repeat the taste trial up to 10 times or until you are sure you like/dislike the food.

   Hint: Many people find the second trial is harder than the first. This is because your brain is learning what to expect. Keep going – it will get easier.

You can try a new food anywhere; many people find it is

actually easier if it is not done at home. This is because we are more likely to stick to old habits or behaviours in our most familiar environment. In fact, many autistic and neurodivergent people find they naturally tend to eat a new food in a new situation without even trying.

Remember Maryam from earlier chapters? Here is more of her story.

Maryam went to a new school, and at lunch on the first day she ate sausages and baked beans. This was a surprise to her parents as she had never eaten these before! Maryam then ate sausages and baked beans for lunch at school every day, but she never ate them at home.

Many autistic and neurodivergent teenagers eat different foods in different places or situations – for example, different foods at home and different foods at school. For most of these young people, these foods never cross over into the other place.

Fact Finder 5.1: New situation, new food

Scientists think that the autistic brain does not always pick up information from one situation and take it to another, which is known as 'generalising'. This can mean that what has been learnt in one situation – such as 'I eat sausages and beans at school' – stays in that situation and does not generalise to other situations, such as 'I also eat sausages and beans at home'.

> This may explain why some autistic and
> neurodivergent people only eat certain foods in
> certain contexts.

Foods that are only eaten in one situation can sometimes
be frustrating for families (it was for Maryam's family), but
it can be helpful too. For example, new foods can be added
every time there is a new situation. This was what happened
to Maryam, who started swimming classes after school and
had chocolate fudge cake in the café afterwards. She never
ate it anywhere else, but it was a new food for her!

Here are some ideas for new situations where a new food
can be added:

- ★ Take a different route home from school/college and
  buy a new food in a café or shop.

- ★ Start a new activity – for example, go swimming and
  have a snack afterwards in the pool café.

- ★ Add a new food each time you start a new year in
  school/college.

- ★ Visit a friend's house and have a new food there.

OK, so when is a good time in your week to try a new food?
Only you can decide this. Most autistic and neurodivergent
people like routines and often find that having a daily or
weekly timetable of events and activities helps them with
anxiety about knowing what is going to happen. Having a
timetable and adding in a regular time for trying the new
food really helps.

Diagram 5.1 shows Rachel's weekly timetable with her taste trials for toast added in.

	Monday	Tuesday	Wednesday	Thursday	Friday	Saturday	Sunday
9:00	School	School	School	School	School	Lie-in	Lie-in
	Art today ☺	Try toast at break 🍞	P.E. today 🙁	History today ☺	Maths today 😠 😣	Saturday club ☺	Try toast 🍞
3:30	Home	Home	Home	Home	Home		
	Try toast 🍞	Swimming ☺	Home-work 🙁	Try toast 🍞	Home-work 🙁	Try toast 🍞	Visit grand-parents ☺
6:00	Tea	Tea	Tea	Tea	Tea	Tea	Tea
10:30	Bed	Bed	Bed	Bed	Bed	Bed	Bed

Diagram 5.1: Weekly timetable

As you can see, Rachel added to her timetable when she planned to try toast. If you look carefully, you'll see Rachel avoided trying toast on days that were already stressful for her, such as when there was a lesson she found hard. Rachel added a tick for each time she successfully tried toast. That helped her know how many times she had tried the toast.

Don't worry if you can't stick to the timetable or if you forget to tick a day. The good news is even if you forget to write it down, your brain will remember you tried the food. Your brain will also remember what the food was like, even if there is a gap before you can try it again. Using an app on a phone or telling a friend are other ways you can record when you've tried something.

Fact Finder 5.2: How many times?

How many times do you think you need to try a new food before your brain learns to like it? Take a guess now...

For babies who are learning about foods, this is easy. They can try a food once or twice and then eat it all the time. For teenagers and adults, it's a different story. Scientists think we actually have to try a food as many as 10–14 times before our brains learn that this food is OK and we like it. That may sound like a lot of times, but if you are motivated, have chosen a food carefully and have prepared, it can be a lot quicker!

Celebrating the small wins

You already know that trying a new food for the first time is hard, especially if you are autistic or neurodivergent, because you have to overcome lots of challenges. Hopefully, this book is helping you do that. A really important way to stay motivated is to celebrate every small win in working towards your goals. Here are some ideas:

★ Reward yourself each time you do a taste trial; this will make it easier to repeat it.

★ A reward could be extra computer time or another enjoyable activity.

★ Tell a friend or family member each time you are successful. Praise helps!

★ Plan a bigger reward for when you've added a new
   food; this will keep you motivated.

So now we've got to the end of Chapter 5, what have we
learnt?

Summary of Chapter 5

✓ What doesn't work and why when trying a
   new food.

✓ What the signs of being ready to try a new
   food are.

✓ Why similar foods or those we are motivated to eat are
   the best choices.

✓ How desensitising to the new food and reducing anxiety
   will prepare you to try it.

✓ What the rules and method of a taste trial are.

✓ How to decide where and when you will try a new food.

✓ Why it can be easier to try a new food in a new location
   or situation.

✓ Why we have to try a new food up to ten times to know
   we like it.

✓ Why celebrating even small wins will keep you motivated.

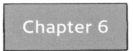

How to Eat with Other People

Reminder of what we learnt in Chapter 5:

- ★ What doesn't work and why when trying a new food.

- ★ What the signs of being ready to try a new food are.

- ★ Why similar foods or those we are motivated to eat are the best choices.

- ★ How desensitising to the new food and reducing anxiety will prepare you to try it.

- ★ What the rules and method of a taste trial are.

- ★ How to decide where and when you will try a new food.

- ★ Why it can be easier to try a new food in a new location or situation.

- ★ Why we have to try a new food up to ten times to know we like it.

★ Why celebrating even small wins will keep you motivated.

Introduction

When we were out as a family, other people's reactions were unhelpful and hurtful for Mum and Dad, and for me when I was old enough to realise what people thought. (Rachel)

I hope no one has ever made you feel awkward or said anything rude about your eating, but I'm afraid that this sometimes does happen. That's one of the reasons I've written about ARFID: to help other people understand that it is a genuine eating problem and not just someone being stubborn or difficult. So if, like Rachel and her family, your eating has caused you stress when you are with other people, or when you are away from home or in public, then this chapter is for you.

This chapter aims to help you understand why being autistic or neurodivergent makes it hard to eat with other people or in public and why social eating situations such as going to a restaurant are often avoided. This chapter will also enable you to explain your eating to other people and give you some ideas to make mealtimes, social eating situations and eating in public easier and perhaps even enjoyable.

In this chapter you will discover:

★ why being autistic or neurodivergent makes eating with other people so hard

★ how social-communication differences impact on eating and how to manage these

★ how to explain your eating issues to other people

★ how to eat more comfortably in public places

★ why sensory overload causes problems at mealtimes and how to manage it

★ how to enjoy eating with other people.

Why is eating with other people so hard?

Read Dan's story.

Dan didn't worry about eating at home because he always knew what he was going to eat and that he was allowed to sit on his own away from other people and their food. When his grandparents visited, Dan had to sit at the table with his whole family, which was really hard. Worse still was when his family went to a restaurant. This made Dan panic. How would he know if his safe foods were on the menu or how noisy it would be?

Does Dan's story sound familiar to you? Do you struggle to eat with other people, perhaps because of food smells or noise, or do you worry about eating somewhere unfamiliar? If so, then you are not alone; many autistic and neurodivergent teenagers feel the same. This is because:

★ 'Social-communication'[1] differences in autism/ neurodivergence make social occasions difficult.

★ Being autistic or neurodivergent makes it difficult to cope in new or unfamiliar places.

★ Eating with other people and/or eating in public can cause sensory 'overload'.

Most autistic and neurodivergent people find it is a combination of these reasons that makes eating with others and in public so much harder for them. The good news is that there are ways you can make this easier. Let's start by working out which social eating situations are hard for you and why.

---

1   Social communication means how we interact and communicate with other people.

Chapter 6 Worksheet 6.1: Which Social Eating Situations Are Hard for Me and Why?

Read the list of common social eating situations. Tick (✓) all that are hard for you and, if you can, write why. Add any other eating situations that you find hard at the end.

1. Mealtimes with my family at home ☐

   Why? . . . .

2. Mealtimes with my family away from home
   (e.g. a relative's house) ☐

   Why? . . . .

3. Eating at school, college or work ☐

   Why? . . . .

4. Eating at a friend's house ☐

   Why? . . . .

5. Eating on holiday ☐

   Why? . . . .

6. Eating at a big event (e.g. a wedding or birthday party) ☐

   Why? . . . .

7. Eating in a restaurant or café ☐

   Why? . . . .

8. Eating with someone I don't know very well (e.g. on a date) ☐

   Why? . . . .

Other difficult social eating situations for me:

1. . . . .

2. . . . .

How many of those situations did you tick? If you ticked all of them, don't worry; these situations are difficult for many autistic and neurodivergent teenagers. This is because you have to deal with the triple whammy of social situations, unfamiliar places and sensory overload. We are going to learn to cope with these one by one, starting with managing social situations that involve eating.

Eating in social situations

Being autistic or neurodivergent means having some differences in how you make sense of the world. This includes how you understand other people and how other people understand you. We call these 'social-communication' differences and they can make friendships and relationships with other people confusing.

Taylor is neurodivergent. Read their story.

Taylor likes being with their friends, but they don't understand when their friends are being sarcastic or making jokes, or why they like to talk about celebrities when Taylor is interested in science. Taylor doesn't know what to do when someone new comes to talk to them, and they get anxious and walk away. This sometimes makes other people think Taylor is rude.

Do you think Taylor is rude? No, me neither. Taylor is neurodivergent and has some social-communication differences, which means it is harder for them to join in with other people's conversations and know how to interact with other people. Instead of being rude, Taylor is actually anxious and needs more support for managing this. Like Taylor, many autistic and neurodivergent people feel stressed in social situations and often avoid them.

Fact Finder 6.1: The double empathy problem

Empathy is the ability to understand and share the thoughts and feelings of another person. When autism was first discovered, scientists thought that only autistic people had problems with empathy. Now scientists know that other people also struggle with empathy and don't always understand how autistic and neurodivergent people think and feel; this is called the 'double empathy problem'. Discovering this is important, because it highlights how everyone needs to try to understand each other, despite our differences.

So, how do social-communication differences affect eating? Across the world and throughout history, social situations often involve food – for example, parties and weddings and mealtimes are often times where people get together to talk and interact. It is easy to see that if you have any social-communication differences, then these situations may be harder. Social eating situations also contain many 'rules' about how we are expected to behave.

Remember Raj from earlier chapters? He is autistic, and this is what happened when he went for a meal with his friend Anya, who is not autistic.

Raj went to dinner with his friend Anya at a restaurant. Raj's food came first so he started eating before Anya got hers. This made Anya cross. During dinner, Anya asked Raj about his new college course, but Raj was too busy eating to answer her. This also made Anya cross, but Raj didn't know why, and this made him sad.

Can you work out why Anya is cross with Raj? Anya was cross because Raj didn't follow the 'rules' of mealtimes, such as waiting until she got her food before eating and talking to her during the meal. However, Raj didn't know or understand these 'rules' and he didn't mean to make Anya cross. Unfortunately, Raj and Anya are caught in the double empathy problem; this means they don't understand each other, and they don't enjoy their meal together.

The good news is that Raj and Anya can make their mealtimes more enjoyable by learning to understand each other a little more. For example:

⭐ Raj can learn more about the 'rules' of mealtimes.

⭐ Anya can learn more about Raj's eating.

These will help solve their double empathy problem. Let's help you, like Raj, understand some of the common social rules of mealtimes.

There are many social rules involved in mealtimes, and these are different depending on history and where you live or your culture. For example, in medieval times it was common to eat only using a knife (forks came much later in history), and in Chinese culture, it is a compliment to burp loudly after eating.

Here are some of the common mealtime 'rules' from UK, European and American culture. I've added some hints to help you make sense of these rules:

⭐ It is polite to talk to other people at the meal.

Hint: Try not to talk about things that might make someone lose their appetite.

⭐ Try not to talk with your mouth full; this is so you don't spit out your food.

Hint: Wait until you have finished chewing and swallowing before speaking.

⭐ It is polite to wait until everyone has their food before starting.

Hint: If you think your food will get cold, then it is OK to ask if you can start.

★ It is rude to use your phone during the meal.

   Hint: Try to talk to the people you are sitting with instead.

★ If cutlery is used in your culture, it is polite to use it rather than your hands.

   Hint: If you struggle with a knife or fork, it is OK to ask for a spoon instead.

★ It is polite to sit at the table until everyone has finished.

   Hint: If you are becoming overloaded, then it's OK to ask to leave.

Sometimes these mealtimes rules may not make sense to you; that's OK. Being able to understand them will make it easier for you to eat with other people if you want to. The most important thing is that you, and those you are eating with, all feel comfortable and relaxed.

Another way for you to feel more comfortable and relaxed at mealtimes is for other people to understand your eating. Unfortunately, sometimes, other people say unhelpful things about eating; here are some comments that have been said to other young people:

Why do you eat the same thing all the time?

Why don't you just eat something else?

Don't be silly; you'll like it!

Just try it; it won't kill you!

Remember, your avoidant eating is not your fault but is connected to being autistic or neurodivergent and to your sensory sensitivities, anxiety and cognitive differences. So, if anyone has ever said anything unhelpful about your eating, then this is not fair. It is also usually not their fault; they simply don't understand why you have issues with food and eating. This is where it can help to explain your avoidant eating to other people.

Remember Dan from earlier chapters? This is what happened to him one day in college.

Dan ate a jacket potato for lunch every day in college. One day the canteen had run out of jacket potatoes and Dan was upset. His friend Lloyd offered him some of his chips instead, but Dan didn't like chips and he walked off. This left Lloyd feeling confused.

Lloyd didn't know that Dan had difficulties with different foods; he just thought Dan really liked jacket potatoes! Once Dan told Lloyd about his ARFID, it was easier for Lloyd to understand and help Dan with his eating. This helped Dan manage and enjoy lunchtimes at college more.

Top Tip: Explaining ARFID

Here is an example of how you can explain your eating to other people. Keep this as a 'script' you can use to tell other people whenever you need to. You could even write it down and show other people instead of telling them.

I am autistic/neurodivergent which means I have some problems with food and eating. These issues are not my fault, but are caused by my sensory sensitivities, my anxiety about new foods and my need for things to be familiar to help me cope. It really helps me if you let me choose my foods and how I eat them, and please don't get upset if I say I can't eat something you offer me. Thanks for listening and understanding me!

How to manage eating in public

Sometimes you may find yourself in a situation where it is not possible to explain your eating to all the people who are there –for example, if you are eating in a public place. Look back now at Worksheet 6.1 and see if you can work out which are the hardest social eating situations for you. Are any of these public eating situations such as eating at school, college or in a café or restaurant? If so, you are not alone. Eating in public often causes anxiety for autistic and neurodivergent people. This is because the situation may be unfamiliar or difficult to predict and cope with.

Read Taylor's story.

Taylor started a course at college. Taylor wasn't worried about the work, but they were worried about what they could eat there. Taylor knew there was a college canteen but didn't know what was on the menu, where they would be able to sit or how many other students would be there.

Have you, like Taylor, worried about eating in a new place, particularly where there will be other people you don't know? Anxiety about new things and places is part of being autistic or neurodivergent, but if you also have avoidant eating, then this anxiety can increase.

Sometimes autistic and neurodivergent people cope with this anxiety by avoiding new places or situations – this is the 'fight, flight, freeze' response we talked about in Chapter 4. This may help you immediately escape a situation that is scary; unfortunately, it can also make the anxiety increase even more. This means you may miss out on interesting and enjoyable experiences and activities. A much better solution is to make a plan for new and unfamiliar situations that involve eating. This is what Taylor did, and it helped them gain some control and reduced their anxiety. Worksheet 6.2 will help you do this.

Chapter 6 Worksheet 6.2: My Public Eating Plan

Choose a public social eating situation that you find difficult – such as eating in a café or restaurant, or at school/college.

Hint: Don't start with the hardest; choose one that you think you may be able to manage with some support.

Write down the situation here:

....

Now tick (✓) which of these ideas would help you cope:

1. Taking a friend/family member with you ☐

2. Preparing by going on a dummy run (e.g. by going there but not eating) ☐

3. Looking at the menu online first ☐

4. Going at the quietest time ☐

5. Taking something to distract yourself with (e.g. a book or tablet) ☐

6. Wearing earplugs/earphones or another sensory support ☐

Add any other ideas here:

1. ....

2. ....

Use these ideas as your plan for eating in public.

Once you've managed one difficult situation, you'll find it easier to manage another. Learning to manage sensory 'overload' will also help you to make eating with others easier.

Managing sensory overload

Remember Stephan from earlier chapters? Stephan is autistic and also has ARFID; this is more of his story.

Stephan hates the college canteen. There were too many people moving around and talking, the chairs and cutlery made an awful scraping noise, and the smells of the food made him feel sick. Stephan was distracted by the bright lights flickering, and he had to escape the canteen to try to find a quiet place to eat on his own.

Stephan is experiencing sensory overload. This happens when your brain and body become full of sensory information and you reach the limit of what you can cope with. Overload usually happens when there is a combination of sensory information, such as too much noise, sights, smells and people. It is easy to see why social eating situations such as dining rooms or restaurants can be a nightmare for autistic or neurodivergent people.

For Stephan, sensory overload triggered his 'fight, flight, freeze' response and made him want to escape or take 'flight' from the college canteen. This is because sensory overload triggers anxiety and panic. Unfortunately, as we become more anxious, our sensory systems become more sensitive, and a vicious cycle can quickly develop. The good news is that it is possible to reduce sensory overload and anxiety to make mealtimes and social eating situations easier.

Tried and tested ideas for overload

The following are ideas from other autistic or neurodivergent teenagers about managing sensory overload – for example, at school or college. They have all been in the same situation as you and they understand that you need some practical ideas that are not too obvious.

- Sit near the door/on the end of a table so it's easy to leave if you need to.

- Tell a friend or an adult how you feel.

- Find a sensory safe space that you can go to (e.g. the library).

- Wear earphones or earplugs to stop noise.

- Wear a hoody or sunglasses to reduce light.

- Use a fiddle gadget or stress ball to help you cope.

Stephan tried some of these ideas and found that by reducing the information from one sense – for example, wearing earplugs/earphones to cut out noise – it was easier for his brain and body to cope with information from his other senses, such as smell. This meant it was easier for him to stay in the situation, instead of having to escape. It is also a good idea to find a sensory 'safe' space you can go to when you just need a break. Remember, Chapter 3 has other ideas for helping you manage sensory sensitivities around foods; you may find it helpful to remind yourself of what you learnt there.

> ## Top Tip: Reasonable adjustments
>
> 'Reasonable adjustments' (RAs for short) are changes that your school, college or work place have to make so that you can access (enter) these places and achieve your best. If you are autistic, neurodivergent or have ARFID, then you are entitled to have RAs if you need them. For example, you might need access to a quiet room to eat or be allowed to wear headphones in class. If you think you need RAs for your eating, then talk to your teacher, lecturer or employer.

Enjoying eating with other people

Let's end this chapter by talking about how you can begin to enjoy mealtimes and eating with other people. Many autistic and neurodivergent teenagers, like Rachel, have told me their eating 'gets in the way' of what they want to do and how they want to live their lives. One of the reasons I have written this book is not just to help you with the difficult things, but to help you reach your 'potential', which means helping you achieve all that you are capable of doing. This includes helping you to enjoy eating with others if this is what you would like to do.

Remember Stephan's story from earlier in the chapter? Stephan found the college canteen so overloading that he had to escape and find somewhere quieter to eat. This is what Stephan said about that.

Because I couldn't stay in the college canteen, I never got to relax with my friends at lunchtime, and it made it harder for me to meet new people.

Stephan's story reminds us that there are some really positive things to be gained from being able to eat with other people. These include:

* ★ enjoying being with your friends

* ★ meeting new people and making new friends

* ★ being able to join in new activities (e.g. going out with friends for a meal)

* ★ learning why other people like different foods

* ★ naturally desensitising to new foods by sitting with people eating them

* ★ naturally reducing sensory overload by learning to cope

* ★ learning about the rules of social situations and becoming more familiar with these

* ★ becoming more comfortable in social situations

* ★ learning more about how to talk and interact with other people

* ★ being able to enjoy holidays or festivals (e.g. Christmas).

You might be able to think of more! Learning to eat with other people or in public means that new activities and experiences can be possible for you, perhaps for the first time. This is why it is such a positive thing to try to achieve. The next (and last) chapter of this book will explore how you can continue to make your eating easier as you become an adult.

So now that we've got to the end of Chapter 6, what have we learnt?

Summary of Chapter 6

✓ Being autistic or neurodivergent makes eating with other people difficult.

✓ Social-communication differences, new situations and overload all cause problems.

✓ The 'double empathy problem' can make social eating situations hard for everyone.

✓ Learning the 'rules' of social eating situations will help you manage mealtimes.

✓ Explaining your eating issues to other people will help them understand.

✓ Anxiety about eating in public can be reduced by making a plan.

✓ Why sensory overload happens and how to manage it.

✓ Why eating with others can be enjoyable and help you achieve your potential.

Chapter 7

Managing My Eating when I'm Older

Reminder of what we learnt in Chapter 6:

- ★ Being autistic or neurodivergent makes eating with other people difficult.

- ★ Social-communication differences, new situations and overload all cause problems.

- ★ The 'double empathy problem' can make social eating situations hard for everyone.

- ★ Learning the 'rules' of social eating situations will help you manage mealtimes.

- ★ Explaining your eating issues to other people will help them understand.

- ★ Anxiety about eating in public can be reduced by making a plan.

- ★ Why sensory overload happens and how to manage it.

- ★ Why eating with others can be enjoyable and help you achieve your potential.

Introduction

> I knew I'd picked the right university when I saw there was a branch of my favourite coffee shop on campus. That meant I knew I could always get my safe foods, and, best of all, everyone else was going there too! (Rachel)

Chapter 7 is the last chapter of this book and is all about managing your eating as you grow up and become an adult. All young people may feel some anxiety about becoming an adult – this is totally normal! However, it is also an exciting time as you learn new skills, have more choice about your life and find out more about who you are.

As Rachel found, learning where you can get your safe foods from when you are an adult is one important independent life skill. Chapter 7 aims to enable you to use what you have learnt so far to help you become more independent with foods and eating as you get older. This will help you live the life you want.

In this chapter you will discover:

★ how to manage your eating when you are more independent

★ how to manage other eating issues and stay in control of your eating

★ how to make sure you stay healthy

★ how other people can support you

★ where to find extra help if you need it.

Managing your eating independently

Getting older and becoming an adult means you are likely to have some different and new experiences, challenges and situations to deal with. If this sounds stressful, that's because if you are autistic or neurodivergent, 'transitions' (moving from one thing to another), such as moving from school to college, can be hard. This is because autism and neurodivergence make it harder to cope with change. If this is difficult for you, then it is really important that you go at your own pace, find support from the right people and use strategies for managing anxiety such as the ones in Chapters 2 and 4. Many people also find that transitions or change are much easier if they have time to prepare and plan.

Remember Maryam from earlier chapters? This is what happened before she started college.

Maryam is starting college in September and was really nervous. Maryam's school teacher and new college tutor got together and organised visits to the college beforehand so Maryam could gradually get used to the new buildings and new staff. This helped reduce Maryam's anxiety, and now college feels really exciting!

Maryam's teacher and tutor helped her plan for the transition to college, which enabled her to be excited about starting instead of feeling worried. This is why making a plan for any changes or transitions really helps as it makes you feel more in control and reduces your anxiety. Worksheet 7.1 will help you identify which changes might be difficult for you in the future and how your eating might be affected.

Chapter 7 Worksheet 7.1: Future Changes and My Eating

Here are some of the different experiences, challenges and situations that may happen as you get older. Next to each are some examples of how your eating might be affected.

Tick (✓) all the ones that would be hard for you and, if you can, write why.

Add any other future situations you think would be hard at the end.

1. Starting college/university – e.g. eating in new places with new people ☐

    Why? ....

2. Starting a job – e.g. you may have to eat lunch at a certain time ☐

    Why? ....

3. Dating/in a relationship – e.g. being embarrassed about your eating ☐

    Why? ....

4. Living independently – e.g. buying and cooking your own food ☐

    Why? ....

5. Socialising with friends – e.g. being invited to a restaurant, café or pub ☐

    Why? ....

Other difficult future situations:

1.  ....

2. ....

3. ....

If you are really worried about changes in the future then make sure you talk to a trusted adult such as a parent or carer, teacher or friend. The good news is that you've already learnt a lot of the skills you will need as an adult to manage your eating; the trick is simply to keep on using them.

Table 7.1 is a reminder of the top 3 key skills you have already learnt in each of the previous chapters. You can use this as a quick guide to what you need to carry on doing in order to be successful at managing your eating independently.

Table 7.1: My Top 3 Skills

	Skill 1	Skill 2	Skill 3
Chapter 1: Why Do I Have Issues with Food and Eating?	I know why I have eating issues	I know which foods are OK for me	I understand ARFID
Chapter 2: Am I Ready to Change My Eating?	I know when to change and when not	I know why I want to change	I can set SMART goals and plan
Chapter 3: Managing My Sensory Differences with Food and Eating	I understand my sensory food issues	I can desensitise to new foods	I know when I am hungry or full
Chapter 4: Managing My Anxiety about Food and Eating	I understand how anxiety causes eating issues	I understand how to challenge anxious thoughts and feelings	I can use relaxation to reduce my anxiety

Chapter 5: How to Try a New Food	I know what doesn't work and why	I know how to choose a new food	I can do a 'taste trial' of a new food
Chapter 6: How to Eat with Other People	I know how 'double empathy' affects eating	I know how to cope in social eating situations	I can manage my sensory overload

Hopefully, by looking at Table 7.1 you can see how many skills you have already learnt by using this book! Now we are going to look at which of these skills will be the most important in enabling you to be independent with foods and eating.

I call this the '5 Point Plan' and it lists the skills you have learnt in order of how important they are in helping you to be independent. This order comes from my experience working with young people with avoidant eating. For example, I learnt that it is difficult to reduce your anxiety about foods if you haven't already worked on your sensory sensitivities. However, if you feel a different order is best for you, then go for it!

Worksheet 7.2 will help you see what you are already able to do and what you still need to work on.

Chapter 7 Worksheet 7.2: My 5 Point Plan

For each skill in bold, you'll see examples of how you can get that skill. Tick (✓) each example once you have achieved it. That way you'll know when you have that skill.

1. **Reduce your sensory sensitivities to different foods.**

   a. Use desensitisation to expose to different foods ☐

   b. Go shopping for different foods ☐

   c. Prepare and cook your own food ☐

2. **Recognise your appetite.**

   a. Schedule regular times to eat every day ☐

   b. Practise noticing what is happening inside your body ☐

   c. Always keep some HCPM foods with you just in case ☐

3. **Reduce your anxiety about foods and eating.**

   a. Recognise the signs of anxiety in your body
      – fight, flight, freeze ☐

   b. Challenge anxious thoughts ☐

   c. Use relaxation to reduce anxiety ☐

4. **Try more new foods.**

   a. Choose foods which are similar or motivating ☐

   b. Practise desensitisation and relaxation before
      trying the food ☐

   c. Do a taste trial and rate what you think of the new food ☐

5. **Eat with other people.**

   a. Learn the rules of social eating and explain your
      eating to others ☐

   b. Plan and prepare for eating in public ☐

   c. Use sensory supports to avoid overload ☐

How to manage other eating issues

Some autistic or neurodivergent teenagers with avoidant eating find they develop other issues around food, and these may cause a problem as they get older.

Read the following stories:

> Dan has ARFID and only eats ten different foods. Dan also eats some non-foods such as paper, cotton wool and cloth.
>
> Raj can't eat if anyone else touches his plate and cutlery. This makes him so anxious that he has to wash them up four times before he can use them.
>
> Maryam's eating is worse when she is anxious. Her mum tries to persuade her to eat, but this makes Maryam refuse even more. Now Maryam can't cope with any demand to eat.
>
> Taylor was worried about exams, and so they began to eat less and exercise more. Taylor has now lost a lot of weight and has now been told by their doctor that they have an 'eating disorder'.

Let's think about these extra eating issues one by one.

Dan eats some non-foods; this is called 'pica',[1] and it sometimes occurs in autistic or neurodivergent people. Many different things may be eaten, such as paper, dirt, cloth, leaves, plastic and wood. Pica may happen because of sensory sensitivities, and it may also happen when people

---

1   Pica is the Latin name for magpie, a bird that collects and eats anything!

are stressed. Sometimes pica is harmless, but other times it can be dangerous, such as if you eat anything sharp or poisonous or something that might make you choke. The most important thing to do if you have pica is to tell the people who support you and your GP or family doctor.

Managing pica

The following are strategies for managing pica:

- Make a list of the non-foods you eat so you can tell the people who support you.

- Tell your GP or family doctor about your pica; they can keep you healthy.

- Ask your GP for a sensory assessment from an occupational therapist (OT).

- Swap non-foods for safe alternatives, such as crunchy foods or a chewy 'buddy'.

- Use strategies for managing your sensory sensitivities and anxiety.

Raj is extremely anxious about people touching his plate and cutlery. This has made Raj 'obsessive' about making sure that everything is really clean. When people become obsessive, they often have unpleasant and repetitive thoughts, such as bad things happening if they don't do a task over and over. Sometimes these behaviours get out of control and take over large parts of a person's day. If you are worried that this is happening to you, it is really important you tell a family member, friend or your GP. This is what Raj did and it helped him get more support.

Maryam becomes anxious when her mum tries to get her to eat. Some autistic and neurodivergent people experience very high levels of anxiety when a 'demand' happens, such as being asked or expected to do something. This is sometimes known as 'Pathological Demand Avoidance' (PDA). When demands happen, people with PDA go into their 'fight, flight, freeze' response. Unfortunately, because eating happens several times a day, people with PDA almost always feel anxious about eating and mealtimes. This was the case for Maryam, but the good news is that there are strategies that helped her and can help you if you are anxious about demands.

The PDA PANDA

PDA can happen when someone feels out of control. The PDA 'PANDA' (PDA Society, 2021) can help you get this control back and feel less anxious. Each letter of the word PANDA stands for a different strategy:

P is for pick one area to work on with food; your SMART goals from Chapter 2 will help.

A is for anxiety; learning to manage this (see Chapter 4) will help you feel in control.

N is for negotiation – e.g. taking responsibility for your eating with people who support you.

D is for demand management – e.g. reducing demands or working out what you can cope with.

A is for adaptation – e.g. other people helping you to be flexible or having a 'plan B'.

Top Tip: Managing demands

People with PDA can also feel really overwhelmed very quickly by tasks – for example, trying to keep up with a SMART goal (see Chapter 2) that you have set yourself. Remember, the most important message of this book is to go at your own pace (it's OK to take a break) and only to make changes when it feels right for you.

When Taylor lost weight, they were told they had an 'eating disorder'. An eating disorder is where someone deliberately restricts what they eat in order to lose weight or perhaps change their body shape. Eating disorders may make a person eat tiny amounts of food, exercise too much or even make themselves sick to get rid of the food they have eaten. People with an eating disorder often have mental health difficulties such as severe anxiety or depression. Autistic or neurodivergent people seem to be more vulnerable to having an eating disorder, and this can develop for a number of reasons – for example, in order to feel in control of difficult situations or feelings, or because they view their body weight or shape differently to how it actually is, which is called 'body dysmorphia'. The good news is most autistic or neurodivergent people with avoidant eating don't develop these types of problems.

Taylor's friend Lindsey noticed that Taylor was eating less at college and was worried. Lindsey encouraged Taylor to tell their tutor who helped Taylor go and see their GP. If you (or someone else) are worried that you may have an eating disorder or that your eating is getting out of control, then it is really important, like Taylor, that you talk to a trusted adult and get the right support quickly. The next section on staying healthy will also help.

Staying healthy

Perhaps the most important part of becoming an adult is learning to look after yourself and stay healthy. Eating plays a big role in staying healthy, so learning how to buy, prepare and cook your own food is important; so is knowing what to do if things go wrong.

The good news is if you are still a teenager, then you have time to learn these life skills. Remember, it is important that you go at your own pace and get the help and support you need along the way.

Top Tips: Going to the supermarket

Going to the supermarket is an important life skill. Supermarkets are also great places to desensitise as you can look at, touch and smell many different types of food. Unfortunately, supermarkets can be difficult if you are autistic or neurodivergent as they can cause sensory overload. The following tips can help:

- Plan ahead – e.g. decide how you will get there.

- Make a list of what you want to buy; this helps you focus.

- Choose a quiet time to go – many supermarkets now have a 'quiet hour'.

- If noise is a problem, wear headphones or ear defenders.

- If light is a problem, try wearing dark glasses.

- Take something with you that helps you relax – e.g. a stress ball/twiddler.

- Take someone with you who can help you notice if you are becoming overloaded.

- Have an exit plan if you get overloaded – e.g. make sure you know how to get out.

- Visiting a smaller shop can help reduce overload.

Learning to cook not only enables you to be more independent but it's also a great way to naturally desensitise as we learnt in Chapter 3.

Read more of Stephan's story.

Mum has always cooked my food, but this changed when I got my evening job as she's still at work when I have to eat and go to my job. I've learnt to cook chicken nuggets myself now. I use the timer on my mobile phone so I know exactly how long they need to be in the oven to be the right shade of brown. (Stephan)

Stephan has learnt to be more independent by using tools such as the timer of his mobile phone to make sure his foods are just right. That way he can take more responsibility for how his foods are cooked and reduce any anxiety.

Another life skill is making sure that you get the right vitamins and minerals to stay healthy. Unfortunately, avoidant eating can make this hard because some food groups, such as vegetables (which contain a lot of the vitamins and minerals we need), are not always eaten. The good news is that some of the common foods we looked at in Chapter 1 are 'fortified', which means extra vitamins and minerals have been added. Eating these foods can help you stay healthy. Learning to take a vitamin and mineral supplement can also help.

Here are some ideas:

1. Check your safe foods to see if they are fortified.

   Hint: Look at the 'nutritional information' on the packaging.

2. Look at different supplements to see if there is a flavour or texture you like.

   Hint: It will be easier if the supplement is similar to a food you already like.

3. Desensitise to the supplement by holding it in your hand and smelling it.

   Hint: Cutting it into smaller pieces may help.

4. When you are ready, try a small piece.

   Hint: This is similar to the method for trying a new food (see Chapter 5).

5. Keep going until you are able to accept the supplement.

   Hint: If the flavour or texture is not right, then pick a different supplement.

6. Schedule a regular time each day to take the supplement.

   Hint: Taking the supplement at the same time as a meal is a good idea.

Another important part of being independent and staying healthy is to know what to do if things start to go wrong with your eating. This includes how to spot the signs that your eating is more worrying or out of control and who you would get support from. This is how a 'safety plan' can help.

✓

Chapter 7 Worksheet 7.3: My Safety Plan

Safety plans are made before anything goes wrong; this helps you know what to do.

Add the details of your plan in the gaps and keep the safety plan just in case.

Hint: The best time for help is when you **start** to worry rather than when eating is already out of control.

1. My eating is OK and I don't need to do anything at the moment.

2. I am worried about my eating. These are the worrying signs:

    ....

    I need to tell a trusted adult. I will tell:

    ....

3. My eating is out of control. These are the signs:

    ....

    I will get help from:

    ....

4. My GP or family doctor's phone number is:........................

Your GP or family doctor will be an important health professional to contact if you are worried or think you need more help. It's a good idea to always make sure you have their phone number handy just in case and that they know you are autistic or neurodivergent. That will help them to help you.

Health and safety reminder

Remember, if you have any food sensitivities, food allergies or intolerances, it is extremely important that you continue to get the right help and support when you are an adult. This includes understanding which foods cause you problems and making sure that your friends, family and health professionals like your GP know you have these issues. A 'Health Passport' (www.autism.org.uk/advice-and-guidance/topics/physical-health/my-health-passport) can help. This is a document you can show health professionals so they can better support you.

Who can help and support me?

Getting the right help and support for your eating is very important as you get older. This is because changing your eating is not easy, and having a support 'network' of people you know and trust means you will have the best chance of success.

Your support network could include:

- ★ family and friends

- ★ teacher, college or university tutor

- ★ youth worker, sports coach, activity group leader

- ★ advocate, support worker, personal assistant/carer.

Worksheet 7.4 will help you decide who can be in your support network.

Chapter 7 Worksheet 7.4: My Support Network

Write the names of people who can go in your support network in the bubble.

Hint: It doesn't matter who goes in as long as they are able to help you.

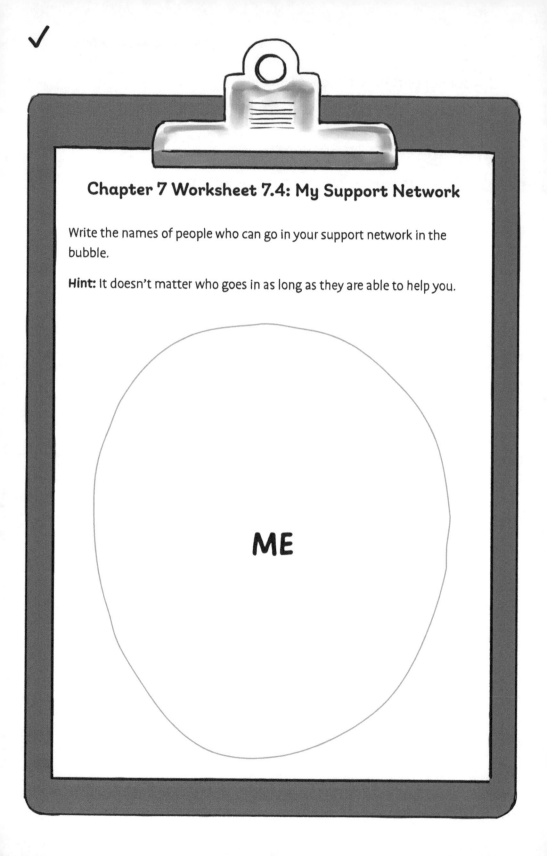

ME

People with avoidant eating sometimes need extra help from health professionals – for example, if you start to develop other eating issues or your eating is out of control. Here are some of the health professionals who work with eating issues and how they can help:

* ★ Clinical psychologist – helps with anxiety and mental health.

* ★ Dietician – helps with nutrition and physical health.

* ★ Gastroenterologist – helps with stomach and bowel problems.

* ★ General practitioner (GP) – helps with general health problems.

* ★ Occupational therapist (OT) – helps with sensory sensitivities and living skills.

* ★ Speech and language therapist (SLT) – helps with social-communication skills.

Your GP or family doctor can also help you find the right professional help if you need it.

Your journey to adulthood

Well done! You've made it to the end of this book. Hopefully, you will have learnt a lot more about why you have food and eating issues and how you can manage these in order to live the life you want. The good news is that most autistic and neurodivergent people, like Dan, Maryam, Rachel, Raj, Stephan and Taylor, find dealing with food issues gets easier as they become adults. That's because you have gained the right skills and motivation to make the changes that are right for you.

As Rachel says:

> There were so many things my diet stopped me from doing. I wanted to do them! (Rachel)

I hope this book has helped you along your journey and I wish you every success.

Now we've got to the end of Chapter 7, what have we learnt?

Summary of Chapter 7

✓ How future planning and reminding yourself of the skills you have learnt will help.

✓ Learning new life skills (e.g. going to the supermarket) will help you be independent.

✓ How to recognise other eating issues and what to do if your eating gets out of control.

✓ How looking after yourself and staying healthy is an important part of independence.

✓ How to make a safety plan to help you cope if things go wrong.

✓ How to identify who can be in your support network.

✓ Where to find extra professional help if you need it.

Appendix 1: Copies of Worksheets to Use Again

Relaxation Rating Scale

Rate how relaxed you feel from 1 (not relaxed) to 10 (very relaxed).

Date: ....

Relaxation method:

1   2   3   4   5   6   7   8   9   10

Date: ....

Relaxation method:..

1   2   3   4   5   6   7   8   9   10

Date: ....

Relaxation method:..

1   2   3   4   5   6   7   8   9   10

Date: ....

Relaxation method:..

1   2   3   4   5   6   7   8   9   10

Taste Trials Rating Sheet

Rate each food you try from 1 (really didn't like) to 10 (really like).

Hint: 3 or less on more than 3 trials means it's time to move on to a new food.

Date: . . . .

Food tried: . . . .

      1   2   3   4   5   6   7   8   9   10

Date: . . . .

Food tried: . . . .

      1   2   3   4   5   6   7   8   9   10

Date: . . . .

Food tried: . . . .

      1   2   3   4   5   6   7   8   9   10

Date: . . . .

Food tried: . . . .

      1   2   3   4   5   6   7   8   9   10

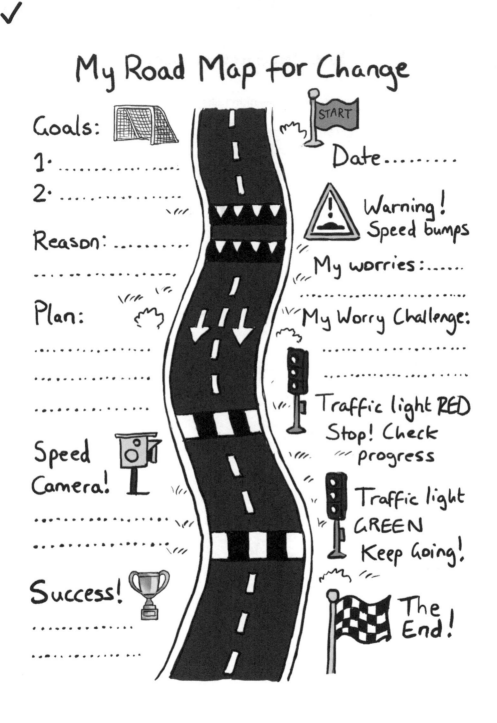

	Monday	Tuesday	Wednesday	Thursday	Friday	Saturday	Sunday
9:00							
3:30							
6:00							
10:30							

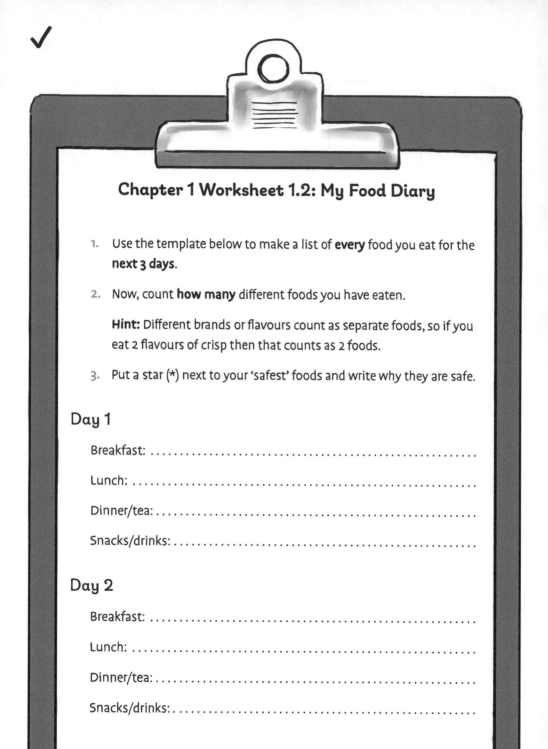

Chapter 1 Worksheet 1.2: My Food Diary

1. Use the template below to make a list of **every** food you eat for the **next 3 days**.

2. Now, count **how many** different foods you have eaten.

   Hint: Different brands or flavours count as separate foods, so if you eat 2 flavours of crisp then that counts as 2 foods.

3. Put a star (*) next to your 'safest' foods and write why they are safe.

Day 1

Breakfast: . . . .

Lunch: . . . .

Dinner/tea: . . . .

Snacks/drinks: . . . .

Day 2

Breakfast: . . . .

Lunch: . . . .

Dinner/tea: . . . .

Snacks/drinks: . . . .

Day 3

Breakfast: ....

Lunch: ....

Dinner/tea: ....

Snacks/drinks: ....

Total number of foods: ....

My safe foods are safe because: ....

....

Chapter 2 Worksheet 2.5: My SMART Goal

Think of a change you want to make about your eating. This will be your SMART goal.

Write it here:

My goal: ....

Now break the goal down by filling in the steps below:

1. **S**pecific: ....

2. **M**easurable:...

3. **A**chievable: ....

4. **R**elevant: ....

5. **T**imely: ....

References

Beck, A.T., Rush, A., Shaw, B. & Emery, G. (1979) *Cognitive Therapy of Depression*. New York: The Guilford Press.

Dahl, R. (2016) *Charlie and the Chocolate Factory*. London: Puffin.

PDA Society (2021) The PDA PANDA. Accessed on 27/09/22 at: www.pdasociety.org.uk/about-us-landing/our-ambassador

Prochaska, J.O. & DiClemente, C.C. (1983) 'Stages and processes of self-change of smoking: Toward an integrative model of change.' *Journal of Consulting and Clinical Psychology 51, 3,* 390–395. http://dx.doi.org/10.1037/0022-006X.51.3.390

Glossary

ADHD Attention Deficit Hyperactivity Disorder

ARFID Avoidant and Restrictive Food Intake Disorder

Autistic/autism Terms to describe Autism Spectrum Disorder (ASD)

Clinical psychologist Health professional who supports people with mental health issues

Cognitive The processes of thinking, reasoning (understanding things) and memory

Cognitive Behaviour Therapy (CBT) A form of talking therapy for anxiety/depression

Contamination A brain process to protect humans from eating anything dangerous

Disgust A brain process to protect humans from eating anything dangerous

DNA/deoxyribonucleic acid Genetic information for inherited traits

Dyslexia A learning difficulty affecting reading and word skills

Dyspraxia A condition affecting coordination and organisational skills

Food allergy A condition where the immune system reacts to certain foods (e.g. nuts, eggs)

Food intolerance A condition where the digestive system reacts to certain foods

Interoception The sense of body awareness

Kilocalories (kcal) A measure of how much energy foods contain

National Health Service (NHS) The UK public health system

Neophobia A developmental stage in humans where unknown food is refused

Neurodivergent/neurodiversity The many ways humans think, learn and relate

Paediatrician Medical doctor who specialises in children and teenagers' physical health

PDA Pathological Demand Avoidance

Proprioception The sense of spatial awareness

Psychiatrist Medical doctor who specialises in mental health

Reasonable adjustments (RAs) Supports required for people to access services

Vestibular The sense of balance

Further Resources

ARFID Awareness UK

UK-based charity raising awareness and providing information about ARFID.

www.arfidawarenessuk.org

Beat

UK-based charity supporting anyone affected by eating disorders or any other difficulties with food, weight and shape.

www.beateatingdisorders.org.uk

More about ARFID for Older Teens and Adults

An additional resource for older teens or adults who may be looking after someone with avoidant eating, from Dr Elizabeth Shea.

www.jkp.com/catalogue/book/9781787758599

National Autistic Society

UK-based charity supporting autistic children, young people and adults and their families. It also provides services for professionals.

www.autism.org.uk

PDA Society

UK-based charity providing information, support and training for parents, carers, teachers and individuals with PDA.

www.pdasociety.org.uk

Scottish Autism

Scottish charity providing autism-specific services. 'Right Click' programmes provide e-training on a range of subjects including eating.

www.scottishautism.org

Young Minds

UK-based charity supporting the wellbeing and mental health of young people.

www.youngminds.org.uk

Index